Soul Pain

Soul Pain

Edited by

Jennifer Tann

CANTERBURY PRESS
Norwich

First published in 2013 by the Canterbury Press Norwich
Editorial office
3rd Floor, Invicta House,
108–114 Golden Lane,
London EC1Y 0TG

Canterbury Press is an imprint of Hymns Ancient & Modern Ltd
(a registered charity)
13A Hellesdon Park Road, Norwich,
Norfolk, NR6 5DR, UK

www.canterburypress.co.uk

British Library Cataloguing in Publication data

A catalogue record for this book is available
from the British Library

978 1 84825 277 6

Typeset by Manila Typesetting Company
Printed and bound in Great Britain by
CPI Group (UK) Ltd, Croydon

Contents

Preface vii
About the Contributors ix

1 Healing and Wholeness 1
Jennifer Tann
2 The Experience of Stroke and the Life of the Spirit 25
Ben de la Mare
3 An Affair of the Heart 37
Brian Andrews
4 Magnificat 50
Jane Tillier
5 A Burden not to be Borne 63
Christopher Finlay
6 The Passing of Time 77
John Clarke
7 Looking at the Bronze Serpent 92
Christopher Collingwood
8 In God I put my Trust 114
Jane Kenchington
9 Invisible Pain 129
Kevin Ellis
10 Snapshots of an Illness 146
Peter Kerr
11 Dark before Dawn 169
Rachel Lewis
12 Lament 184
Gordon Mursell

Index 200

Preface

The seed for this book was sown one Good Friday. Our parish priest was sick, having undergone major heart surgery. During the three-hour service I became aware of his presence, with us but not among us, sitting on a ledge with his back to the north wall of the church, weeping. Some years later I became work consultant to a priest with a terminal illness and we began to explore the theme of the sick priest in public ministry: each person's unique experience; whether the priest is 'on duty' in hospital; the role of lament; prayer by proxy; ritual; comfort; seeking wholeness. It seemed that a collection of essays might make a contribution to all who experience or have experienced serious illness, whether priest or lay, as well as to those in ministerial training, lay church workers, and medical professionals. We dedicate this book to all who seek to enable the sick to find wholeness and healing.

Jennifer Tann

About the Contributors

Brian Andrews read Theology at Keble College,Oxford, before training at the College of the Resurrection, Mirfield. He was ordained in 1964, and has served in the parishes of the Isle of Dogs, St Mary, Hemel Hempstead and St Lawrence, Abbots Langley, becoming Rural Dean of Watford. He has been Chair of Diocesan Synod, Member of General Synod, and is Canon Emeritus of St Albans Cathedral. He is the author of *Training Incumbents*. He retired to Gloucestershire in 2005. His interests are family, music, sport and natural history.

John Clarke has been Dean of Wells since 2004. After university at Oxford and Edinburgh, his work has included being principal of a theological college, a parish priest in the diocese of Southwark, and a provincial role within the Scottish Episcopal Church, as well as a year of study in Greece. He is married to Cressida Nash and they have three grown-up children. John also acts as a spiritual director and is a church commissioner.

Christopher Collingwood is Rector of Minchinhampton with Box and Amberley, and Area Dean of Stroud, in the Diocese of Gloucester. He has degrees in music and theology from the universities of Birmingham and Oxford respectively, as well as a PhD from the University of London. He has served as a priest in a variety of contexts: parish, cathedral and school. He is involved in the work of several committees in the Diocese of Gloucester and chairs the Bishop of Gloucester's Worship, Prayer and Spirituality Group.

Kevin Ellis is Parish Priest at Bartley Green in the Diocese of Birmingham, having previously been team vicar of three parishes in Carlisle Diocese. He studied for his BA at Newcastle University, holds a PhD in New Testament Studies, and is committed to making the Bible accessible to those he serves. He is married, has a son and two bouncy lurcher dogs, which contribute to keeping him sane.

Christopher Finlay is an NSM in the South Cotswold Team Ministry. He spent nearly twenty years in Reader Ministry in five dioceses, while pursuing a career in financial services, before being ordained in 1998. His ministry has been largely rural parochial ministry and in Diocesan Administration, including chairing the DBF. He is an honorary Canon of Gloucester Cathedral. He is married to Patty and has two married children. He has had cancer since 2002.

Jane Kenchington read chemistry at Hull University, followed by teaching in Ghana and Northamptonshire. After training at Westcott House, she was ordained deacon in Gloucester Cathedral in 1990 and was ordained priest in 1994. Jane has worked in parochial ministry; she taught liturgical studies for WEMTC and was Dean of Women Clergy and Canon in the Diocese of Gloucester before taking up her present post as Rector of the Sodbury Vale Benefice. She has an MA in Applied Theology. She is married to Richard and they have two teenage daughters.

Peter Kerr is a priest in the Diocese of Worcester, having previously been Adult Education and Theological Training Officer in the Diocese. He studied for his BA and MPhil at Edinburgh. After training in Northen Ireland he lectured at Lincoln Theological College. He is married to Diane and they have four children and three grandchildren. He finds gardening, wild swimming and wine-making immensely healing. He is an honorary Canon of Worcester Cathedral.

Rachel Lewis is Rector of Walbury Beacon Benefice in Oxford Diocese. She studied Theology at Durham University followed by a PGCE and MSc, taught music and then trained at Salisbury and Wells Theological College. She served her curacy in Swansea in 1986, undertook two successive university chaplaincies before being ordained priest in 1994. She has held benefice posts in Bristol, Limerick and South Wales. She enjoys music, story-telling, fabric, reading and gardening.

Ben de la Mare studied clarinet before classics and then theology at Oxford University (1959–63). He was ordained priest in Newcastle-upon-Tyne in 1966, was chaplain at Trinity College Cambridge 1968–73, returning to the north-east as vicar of St Gabriel's Heaton (Newcastle) and then St Oswald's Durham. While at St Oswald's he was part-time chaplain at Durham Prison, at various schools, and latterly (1995–2005) at Collingwood College. He had a haemorrhagic stroke in January 2002, and a second in February 2009. He died on 29 October 2009.

Gordon Mursell was brought up in Sussex, studied music in Rome and history and theology at university before being ordained. He worked as a curate in Liverpool, a vicar in London, a theological teacher in Salisbury, a team rector in Stafford, a cathedral dean in Birmingham and a bishop back in Stafford. His wife Anne is a consultant psychiatrist and they live in south-west Scotland. He has written a number of books on spirituality.

Jennifer Tann is Professor Emerita of Innovation at Birmingham University, having held prior academic appointments at the universities of Aston and Newcastle-upon-Tyne. She has been Visiting Professor at the University of New South Wales and has undertaken university lecture tours in the USA and Canada. She was a member of Birmingham Cathedral Chapter. Now resident in Gloucester Diocese she is a member of Bishop's Council and General Synod. She has written a number of books and academic papers.

Jane Tillier is Priest-in-Charge of Barlaston, Ministry Development Adviser for the Stafford Episcopal Area, Diocesan Adviser for Women in Ministry and an honorary Prebendary of Lichfield Cathedral. Before training at Ripon College Cuddesdon, she completed a PhD in Spanish and was lay chaplain at Jesus College, Cambridge. Since being ordained deacon in 1991 and priest in 1994 she was been variously curate in Sheffield, on the staff of Gloucester Cathedral, parish priest in a number of parishes in Lichfield Diocese and Chaplaincy Team Leader at a hospice.

1

Healing and Wholeness

Jennifer Tann

To live abundantly in the knowledge that we are wholly loved by God does not immunize us from pain and desolation and, where there is a terminal prognosis, we are not freed from suffering and sorrow but are enabled to be healed into wholeness and to integrate death into a narrative of hope. Jesus' agonizing cry from the cross is a powerful exemplar and endorsement of the role of lament in suffering. The exhortation to 'keep awake . . . for you know neither the day nor the hour' (Matthew 25.13) instructs Christians to focus on *being* in present time and this takes on a special significance in illness, whether it is terminal or not and the potential for each person to achieve wholeness through healing in body, soul and spirit.

When we feel well, we may enjoy the illusion that we are in control of our lives; that we can predict/plan for next month/next year and even beyond. And, while natural disasters – and human-made ones – remind us of the seeming randomness of events that can radically change people's lives or, indeed, of the car crash that might happen tomorrow, we tend to continue to believe that 'all shall be well'. John Hull experienced his loss of sight as 'an expression of separation'[1] and the onset of serious illness can be sudden as it was for Christopher Finlay, Rachel Lewis, Peter Kerr and Jane Kenchington, who all contribute to this book. It can seem to be random. There may be an initial response 'Why me?' The individual may experience a tension in their personal story between a hoped-for future and a different reality now framed by

1 John Hull, *In the Beginning there was Darkness*, SCM Press, 2001, p. 1.

suffering. David Stancliffe, preaching at the Salisbury Chrism Service on his return to duty following serious illness, referred to the epistle for the day: 'We have this treasure in earthen vessels' (2 Corinthians 4.74), adding 'and don't I know it. It's one thing to preach about earthen vessels, it's quite another to find that you are one . . . I think I've discovered quite a lot about being a "cracked pot" since last year.'[2]

The priest or minister encounters illness, suffering and grieving in the pastoral work of their ministry. They will have encountered heart-breaking incidents of illness occurring before what is thought to be a normal lifespan: still-birth, a child cancer patient, a road accident, a bright young person off to university who is struck down. Robert McCrum experienced a severe stroke at the age of forty-two and, when he had sufficient movement to keep a diary, he wrote: 'my instinct during these days has been that of the beetle or cockroach without a leg, flailing helplessly and covered in dirt, on the brink of extinction.'[3] The incidence of serious illness in a more normal lifespan is little easier to bear. What happens when the priest falls ill, continuing in public ministry in the knowledge that he/she has a potentially life-threatening condition? (S)he may reassure others that God cares, while secretly feeling abandoned, let down. The inexplicable apparent randomness of serious illness is hard to bear 'Where (has) the clear flightpath gone? Where (is) the pilot? Even sophisticated believers can lose their balance when faced with serious ill health.'[4] While undertaking pastoral care for others may be some preparation,[5] it is very different from personally experiencing serious or terminal

2 David Stancliffe, sermon preached at Chrism Eucharist, 2009.

3 Robert McCrum, *My Year Off*, Picador, 1998, p. 59.

4 John Pritchard, *God Lost and Found*, SPCK, 2011, p. 29.

5 A fairly recent assessment in the USA suggests, however, that priests are not much better prepared than any other American to support the chronically ill through death and dying, see Abigail Rian Evans, 'Healing in the Midst of Dying . . .', in John Swinton and Richard Payne (eds), *Living Well and Dying Faithfully*, William B. Eerdmans Publishing Co, 2009, p. 168.

illness. 'Death can't be talked down, or parlayed into anything; it simply declines to come to the negotiating table.'[6]

In the essays that follow there is no suggestion that priests/ministers necessarily think or feel differently from others when seriously ill. Their priestly calling has, however, enabled them to articulate theologically what others, but not all, may find some difficulty in expressing. Priests live with Old and New Testament healing stories; they have wrestled with the apparent randomness of healing by Jesus. They acknowledge that a theology of healing is embedded in Shalom which has to do with holiness and a right relationship with God; that peace, comfort, community, and justice emerge but are not dependent upon cure.[7] This was emphasized in the Report of the Archbishop's Commission on Healing. Christian healing does not necessarily relate to the restoration of function but to the possibility of fulfilling the purpose for which humankind was created. 'There is no one who cannot feel God's healing embrace. There is no one to whom the Holy Spirit of love and compassion is not made available. There is no one, finally, whom God has not already reached, in Jesus Christ; Christian faith is "not problem-solving but mystery encountering".'[8] As the late Daniel Hardy wrote, 'For the church to begin to heal, the pastor must be transformed, from one who actively pastors . . . to one who serves as representative of the congregation's woundedness and who opens himself (sic) to becoming an agent of whatever transforming and healing spirit makes itself known within the life of the church.'[9] Priests are 'chosen,

6 Julian Barnes, *Nothing to be Frightened of*, Vintage Books, 2009, pp. 69, 71. Or, as Miles Kington wrote in his memorably titled book, *How shall I tell the Dog?*, Profile Books, 2008.

7 John Swinton and Richard Payne, 'Christian Practices and the Art of Dying Faithfully', in *Living Well and Dying Faithfully*, p. xxii.

8 *A Time to Heal, Report for the House of Bishops in the Healing Ministry*, Church House Publishing, 2000, pp. 24, 129.

9 Daniel W. Hardy with Deborah Hardy Ford, Peter Ochs and David F. Ford, *Wording a Radiance: Parting Conversations on God and the Church*, SCM Press, 2010, p. 107.

called, anointed and set among God's people to love, serve and cherish them in the paths of righteousness and peace'.[10] There is no suggestion here that, as men and women of God, priests feel that they should be, or have been, treated differently. But they articulate the questions we all may ask when we or our loved ones are struck down with serious illness. The onset of sudden illness is transformative; as David Stancliffe reminded his listeners, 'It's about what I am becoming, and what I am now able to be for you: a human person, fully alive, but rather different, and keenly invested in believing that this may be possible for you too . . . a real re-appraisal of what you might creatively be becoming is something we could all encourage in and for each other.'[11]

Accounts of healing in the Bible

A central part of Jesus' ministry was healing the sick; healing and preaching being revelations of the mercy and power of God at work. Healing was a demonstration of Jesus' God-given authority. He is said to have healed many, but he did not heal all the sick whom he encountered (e.g. one man among the many at Bethzatha pool; John 5.2–9). Jesus healed both out of deep compassion for the sick and as a means of demonstrating that 'the Son of Man has authority on earth to forgive sins'(Mark 2.9–11; Matthew 9.1–8, 27–31; Luke 5.18–26). In the majority of episodes recorded in the New Testament the recipient was physically healed from their disease first followed, on occasion, by Jesus' affirmation of the role that the recipient's faith had played (Luke 8.40–49). We are not always told if the sick person had faith; sometimes it was the petitioner on their behalf. Some were healed or raised by Jesus' touch (John 9. 1–7, 11.43; Luke 7.11–17), yet others were healed or raised at a distance (Matthew 8.5, 9.18–23; John 7.1). When the imprisoned John

10 Stancliffe, sermon.
11 Stancliffe, sermon.

the Baptist sent word to Jesus, asking for confirmation that he was the Promised One, Jesus replied, 'Go and tell John what you hear and see; the blind receive their sight, the lame walk, the lepers are cleansed, the deaf hear, the dead are raised' (Matthew 11.4–5). Healing was the clearest evidence of God's Son in the world.

Healing episodes are recorded in the Old Testament, although less frequently. One of the most explicit is Elijah's petition for the widow of Zarephath's dead son: 'O Lord my God, let this child's life come in to him again' and the child was healed (1 Kings 17.17–24). Elisha, similarly, prayed for the raising of a dead child 'putting his mouth upon his mouth, his eyes upon his eyes, and his hands upon his hands' and the Shunammite woman's son lived (2 Kings 4.32–34). Barren women were healed and bore children (Genesis 21.1–7; Judges 13.2–24) and lepers were made whole (Exodus 4.1–7; Numbers 12.1–15; 2 Kings 5.1–14). Isaiah prophesied that when the Lord is petitioned he 'will listen to their supplications and heal them' and, in the fulfilment of his promise, 'the eyes of the blind shall be opened, and the ears of the deaf unstopped; then the lame shall leap like a deer, and the tongue of the speechless sing for joy' (Isaiah 19.22; 32.3–4; 33.24; 35.5–6). Jesus reminded his hearers that Isaiah claimed he had been anointed to proclaim release of captives 'and recovery of sight to the blind' (Luke 4.16–27). Old Testament accounts of healing conclude with Malachi's prophesy that 'the sun of righteousness shall rise, with healing in its wings' (Malachi 4.3).

During his ministry Jesus gave power and authority to the disciples to drive out demons and to cure diseases (Luke 9.1), linking the charism of healing and working miracles with the ministry of preaching. In Mark's account they were sent out in pairs (Mark 6.7), the action of a teacher who understood the need for mutual support. Jesus intervened when the disciples wanted a man who was not one of their number to cease driving out demons in his name; 'anyone who has faith in me will do what I have been doing. He will do even greater things than these because I am going to the Father' (John 14.12, NIV). Shortly after his resurrection Jesus charged his disciples to 'preach the gospel to all creation', adding that, among the signs which would follow those who believe would be that demons would be cast out in his name, and 'they will lay hands on the sick and the sick will be made well' (Mark 16.15–18).

After Jesus' ascension and upon receiving the gift of the Holy Spirit, the disciples, having witnessed the significance of healing in conversion, undertook healing as part of their task of spreading the gospel, as did Paul. Peter's healing of a crippled man at the temple gate is the story of a gift which was unasked for and unanticipated (Acts 3.6–8). People were even healed by Peter's shadow falling on them (Acts 5.15–16). Crowds were amazed at Philip 'delivering those with evil spirits and healing the crippled and paralytic' (Acts 8.6–8), while 'God did extraordinary miracles through Paul, so that even handkerchiefs and aprons that he had touched were taken to the sick and their illnesses were cured and the evil spirits left them' (Acts 19.11–12 NIV). Nevertheless, death is part of the human condition and Paul writes of 'the sufferings of this present time' which 'are not worth comparing with the glory about to be revealed' (Romans 8.18), and while all will die 'so all will be made alive in Christ' (1 Corinthians 15.22).

Healing and wholeness today

In the early twentieth century, some two thousand years later, severe illnesses were thought to stem from the repression of emotions. Katherine Mansfield believed, in the 1920s, that she could be cured of her advanced tuburculosis if only she could heal the self and, when Susan Sontag first wrote of her cancer in 1978, there was a sense of shame in illness as metaphor, as dis-ease. A decade later, healed of her cancer, she asserted that illness was not a metaphor, nevertheless: 'It is hardly possible to take up one's residence in the Kingdom of the ill unprejudiced by the lurid metaphors by which it has been landscaped.'[12]

---

12 Susan Sontag, *Illness as Metaphor and Aids and its Metaphors*, Penguin, 1977, 2nd edn, 1991, p. 3.

Part of a parish priest's (or hospital chaplain's) work is visiting the sick and dying; but what is a healing ministry in contemporary society? While healing ministry does, for some priests, particularly from the charismatic evangelical wing of the Church, mean physical cure, for others it concerns wholeness.[13] Healing, nowadays, may be revealed in many ways: extraordinary cures, recoveries more rapid than expected, and 'from prolonged sufferings gradually accepted with Christ-like patience and joy to deaths peacefully entered in the hope of God's mercy and love'.[14] James Casson, a young Christian family doctor wrote, 'Release came with the realization that the whole issue was out of my hands . . . The great joy was that the Lord was at the tiller, his face gently smiling and his eyes twinkling as he quietly guided me to my destination. Was I healed? Yes, I believe I was.'[15] F. F. Bosworth (whose book *Christ the Healer* has been continuously in print since it appeared in 1924) claimed: 'The greatest barrier to the faith of many seeking bodily healing in our day is the uncertainty in their minds as to it being the will of God to heal all . . . there is much in modern theology that keeps people from knowing what the Bible clearly teaches – that healing is provided for all.'[16] Anthony de Mello reminded Jesuit retreatants that petition was the only prayer that Jesus taught his disciples. But the person must ask in faith, 'never doubting, for the one who doubts is like a wave of the sea, driven and tossed by the wind'; the doubter 'must not expect to receive anything from the Lord' (James 1,5–8).[17] Jesus, when teaching petitionary prayer to the disciples, emphasized the element of faith: 'whatever you ask for in prayer, believe that you have received it, and it will be yours' (Mark 11.24). Paul

13 Michael Baughen, *The One Big Question*, CWR, 2010.

14 *A Time to Heal*, p. 23.

15 Quoted in David Atkinson, *The Church's Healing Ministry*, Canterbury Press, 2011, pp. 2–3.

16 F. F. Bosworth, *Christ the Healer*, Grand Rapids, Chosen, 1924, 2000, p. 49.

17 Anthony de Mello, *Contact with God: Retreat Conferences*, Anand, 1997, p. 53.

encourages: 'make your requests known to God in prayer and petition with thanksgiving. Then the peace of God, which is beyond our utmost understanding, will keep guard over your hearts and your thoughts, in Christ Jesus (Philippians 4.6–7). Nevertheless, David Atkinson warns of a 'manipulative style' of ministry which raises expectations of miraculous cures: 'The key thing about a miracle . . . is not its cleverness, but the fact that it is a breaking-in of the new Age of God's kingdom into this present one.' A miracle cure – and they do happen – is not a breaking of the laws of nature but, rather, something which we do not regard as natural; 'miracles are signs of God's new order in our world, which cannot be programmed or manipulated, but to which we can be open with prayerful expectation and gratitude'.[18]

During his experience of cancer, David Watson received a healing visit from three evangelists from the USA and both he and they were sure that he had been physically healed. Until the final few weeks of his life, Watson believed in the possibility that he could be physically healed but 'I am getting used to people looking at me as a dying man under sentence of death (although) nothing is certain . . . Everything is a matter of faith.'[19] De Mello questioned why we do not witness the kinds of miracles experienced by the early Church: 'we have never needed miracles so badly; and the reason why we don't have more is that we just don't expect miracles to happen; our faith is very low'.[20] Others, however, 'are able to use their sickness, their pain, even their dying as a time for growth and a new-found trust in the God who holds us in death as in life and will not let us go. And perhaps they are not as rare as we think.'[21]

18 David Atkinson, *The Church's Healing Ministry*, Canterbury Press, 2011, p. 84.

19 David Watson, *Fear No Evil: A Personal Struggle with Cancer*, Hodder and Stoughton, 1984, p. 152. See also David Watson, *Jehova Rapha: God who Heals*, Gilead Books, 2010.

20 De Mello, *Contact with God*, p. 54.

21 Michael Mayne, *A Year Lost and Found*, Darton, Longman and Todd, 1987, p. 71.

Healing, then, concerns seeking a right relationship with God and from this emerges holiness, peace, comfort and, sometimes but by no means always, physical healing. As Paul reminds us, 'We do not live to ourselves, and we do not die to ourselves. If we live, we live to the Lord, and if we die, we die to the Lord; so then, whether we live or whether we die we are the Lord's' (Romans14.7–8). When Peter Chicken, a priest dying of cancer, collapsed at home, he was carried to bed and his wife thought that he had died. After a little while he unexpectedly opened his eyes and, with a radiant smile, said, 'Now I know it's true', before passing into unconsciousness.[22]

Jesus had a remarkable healing ministry yet God, apparently, fails to answer all prayers for cure and there is little record in the Bible of the spiritual health or subsequent situation of those whom Jesus healed. While recognizing that to continue in relative physical and mental health is a God-given desire, a deeper need is tranquillity, healing in the deepest sense of becoming more whole: 'It will bring us to the source of intimacy and beauty that we long for; it brings us to God.'[23] Priests in their pastoral role have, on a number of occasions, to address the seeming randomness of physical healing. Why are some – with or without faith – physically healed, while among others with faith some are physically healed and others are not? What is to be said to the person who is ill; to their loved ones? And, if the priest falls seriously ill, is this a particular challenge to faith? Does he/she feel abandoned, angry? Is there a sense of feeling distant from God? Peter Chicken wrote a 'last letter' to his parish in which he quoted part of his final sermon, given on Easter Day:[24]

> Our greatest fear is the unknown – and death is an unknown – or at least it was. We now know that death is but a stage in

22 I am indebted for this story to Mrs Pat Chicken.

23 Barbara Baisley, *No Easy Answers, Living with Suffering*, new edn, Christine Worsley, ed., Inspire, 2007, p. 97.

24 Peter Chicken, *A Last Letter?* Distributed on Easter 2, 2006. Peter died on 6 June 2006.

life – and when we step through that door we become everything that we can ever be. The way to our great freedom is through an empty cross and an empty tomb.

Gethsemane and Good Friday are never far away from priests' meditations on their sickness. There are stories of the faithful being asked to go further than they believed they had strength, let alone inclination: 'When you were young you fastened your belt about you and walked where you chose; but when you are old you will stretch out your arms, and a stranger will bind you fast, and carry you where you have no wish to go' (John 21.18). Daily worship and prayer (and some priests were greatly aware of their dependence upon others for this in times of acute pain and distress) does not prevent the experience of doubts, but the core of spiritual formation that comes from a life lived in discipleship may enable a person to begin to make sense of their suffering at a time when 'logic easily overwhelms hope'.[25] Ben de la Mare, one of the contributors to this volume, came to recognize, in his brokenness that it was Christ himself who stood across his path saying, 'I have been here. Don't be afraid of the darkness.' We are not expected to bear our pains unaided; we are expected *not* to have the strength; this is something that comes from God.[26]

Writing on healing and wholeness

A number of books have appeared in the past ten years or so in which priests (and a few laypeople of faith) have addressed the question of their illnesses. Some authors (e.g. Barbara Baisley; David Watson[27]) adopt a narrative interwoven with theological reflection from the first realization that something is wrong to the conviction that they will be physically healed, or to an acceptance that the illness is terminal. Others present

25 Swinton, 'Practising the Presence of God . . .', p. 15.
26 Anthony de Mello, *Contact with God*, p. 32.
27 Baisley, *No Easy Answers*; Watson, *Fear no Evil*.

parallel accounts: a chronological account is mirrored in a second section of theological reflection (e.g. Michael Mayne's account of ME[28]). For some writers, death itself is the healing gift as s(he) anticipates release from chronic pain and suffering and finds peace. And a number of contributors to this book draw attention to the ritual and gift of touch; of someone sitting alongside to express what words cannot.

Margaret Spufford wrestled 'as a non-theologian' (but a deeply perceptive and insightful person of faith) in feeling 'helpless to resolve this tension between religious belief and observed fact'. 'It seemed', she wrote, 'so improbable that anything worthwhile could be brought out of all this pain, that I am not infrequently filled by amazement and gratitude that anything constructive could emerge from such unpropitious beginnings and roots so damaged.'[29] She was living with her own disabling skeletal disintegration, a severe form of osteoporosis, while caring for a very disabled daughter. Confronting the illness and owning it 'is to come to accept with some kind of loving tolerance . . . that the deficiencies which frightened you remain, that you will never feel safe or adequate . . . but that you are still usable and can still be used'.[30] This was a point made by Barbara Baisley: 'Through the experience of cancer, some of the phantasy images of myself as "super-vicar-woman" have gone. What I am being asked to do is to accept my humanity, to understand that being afraid is acceptable to God. And so, when I remember, also to me.'[31] The burden of responsibility for others' reactions is one to which several authors allude in this book, in particular the tension between being both priest and patient (Jane Kenchington, Peter Kerr and Jane Tillier). Gillian Rose acknowledged that 'what people now seem to find most daunting with me . . . is not my illness and possible death, but my accentuated being; not my morbidity but my renewed

28 Mayne, *A Year Lost and Found*.

29 Margaret Spufford, *Celebration*, Fount, 1989, p. 18.

30 Spufford, *Celebration*, p. 26.

31 Baisley, *No Easy Answers*, p. 20.

vitality'.[32] She was clear that she needed to feel in control of what information was given out and that, first, she needed to make 'the initially unwelcome event one's inner occupation . . . in ill-health as in unhappy love, this is the hardest work. It requires taking in before letting be.'[33]

In the Gospels Jesus seems to see sickness as an evil (Matthew 13.28); for Paul the 'thorn . . . in the flesh' remained, despite his thrice-times entreaties 'for power is made perfect in weakness' (2 Corinthians 12. 7–9). It is perhaps that, while bad health is not willed by God, all things remain within his authority and may be part of his larger purpose, although we may not perceive it. It is then that reminders of the unshakeable power of God's love are a deep comfort: 'I have loved you with an everlasting love' (Jeremiah 31.3). Barbara Baisley was comforted by Mother Julian: 'He did not say, "You shall not be tempest tossed . . . you shall not be discomforted." But he said, "You shall not be overcome."'[34] Harold Kushner, a rabbi, had a three-year-old son who was diagnosed with a degenerative disease, which meant not only that the child would die in his early teens, but that he had 'rapid ageing' and would resemble a little old man while still young. A year and a half after his son died aged fourteen, Kushner wrote of the randomness of suffering in the world, emphasizing that such episodes are not some form of punishment.[35] His book began with the passage in 2 Samuel (12.19–23) in which David explains why, on the death of his child, he ate: 'Now that he is dead why should I fast? Can I bring him back again? I shall go to him; but he will not return to me.' Frances Young, whose eldest son is severely disabled, travelled a path of bleak despair in which her faith was severely tested. She came to realize that 'the redeeming Christ becomes the *alter ego* of all humanity, but can only become so when we

32 Gillian Rose, *Love's Work*, Vintage, 1997, p. 72.

33 Rose, *Love's Work*, p. 91.

34 Baisley, *No Easy Answers*, p. 50.

35 Harold S. Kushner, *When Bad Things Happen to Good People*, Random House, 1981.

admit our utter vulnerability, our "handicap"'.[36] When Simon Bailey, an openly gay parish priest, was diagnosed HIV positive in 1985, despite feeling 'fit and healthy and well' he found himself 'from then on living in the face of dying'. He wrote of having no idea what to do with this information 'I would look at it, hold it up, walk round it – "you might soon be dead" – but it didn't sink in.' Then there were times when 'it would overwhelm me . . . I do things . . . and suddenly something sinks away – the possibility, it yawns and gapes, an abyss'.[37]

Depression is something that the individual may slide into without recognizing what is happening until the 'hordes of demons swarm . . . back gleefully', and 'the black tangle of misery, anxiety, rage, grief, terror, panic, loss, jumbled up into a churning state' threaten to overwhelm.[38] Perhaps the seductive tunnel of 'long velvet darkness'[39] is experienced, but also sheer anarchy; as Christopher Collingwood, one of the contributors to this book, wrote: 'I became painfully aware that the more effort I put into getting better the worse I became.'[40] No clear answer to the question 'Why me?' may be presented but asking the question not once but many times can lead to self-discovery. 'Although I never wanted to embark on this journey of self-examination, I am grateful now for having made it and even for having to make it again periodically.'[41] In this regard, the sick priest may take on a significant role in becoming both healer and teacher for he/she (in common with all humankind) has a responsibility to be a steward of creation and may share

36 Frances Young, *Face to Face: A Narrative Essay in the Theology of Suffering*, T&T Clark, 1990, p. 137.

37 Simon Bailey, *The Well Within: Parables for Living and Dying*, Darton, Longman and Todd, 1996, pp. 3–4.

38 Justine Picardie, the *Times* 2, 1 May 2010, quoted in John Pritchard, *God Lost and Found*, SPCK, 2011, p. 29.

39 Picardie, *The Times*, p. 29.

40 Christopher Collingwood, *The Divine Dance of Love: Sharing in the Mystery of Christ*, Canterbury Press, 1996, p. 105.

41 Baisley, *No Easy Answers*, pp. 50–1.

in bringing spiritual and emotional healing in the midst of pain.[42]

Gethsemane and Good Friday appear in many meditations by the sick. The God who is in the world's agony and who is also beyond the world; the suffering God who bears us in his arms holding us to the end of time; 'It is all sorrow, all suffering, all brokenness. We have gone out with Jesus into the dark, into the night.'[43] Despair, as well as physical agony, can seem to reach the unbearable. And yet, when Margaret Spufford was dropped, albeit by only a few inches, when being stretchered by ambulance men, it was 'quite extraordinarily at that moment of unreachability, I had suddenly been aware even as I screamed, of the presence of the Crucified. He did not cancel the moment, or assuage it, but was inside it.'[44] The final words of Michael Mayne's moving account of ME (before a name was put to the disease) acknowledge both the cost and gift of illness: 'I now know a little of what it feels like to live in the shadow-land with those whose lives are diminished; and in my better moments I am glad to have done so.'[45]

Receiving health news which states that a condition is inoperable or incurable presents a crisis situation. For some, it is said, this initially triggers relief in the knowing. But, for many, hearing the prognosis leads to shock and fear; not just for themselves but for partners and family members. This is coupled with a sense of responsibility for being the source of that shock to them, a not inconsiderable additional burden. Barbara Baisley wrote of her concern for her husband who would be widowed in his 50s; Jane Kenchington, in this volume, writes of praying to be spared long enough to see her children into young adulthood; Brian Andrews writes of his weeping son; Christopher Finlay of concern for his wife. Shock, may be followed by denial and this may, particularly, be the case where the individual looks (and, possibly, feels)

42 Rian Evans, 'Healing in the Midst of Dying . . .', pp. 173–4.
43 Michael Perham, *The Sorrowful Way*, SPCK, 1998, p. 82.
44 Spufford, *Celebration*, p. 38.
45 Mayne, *A Year Lost and Found*, p. 82.

well. Indeed an additional burden to a person with a chronic illness who looks well is that people keep commenting on this to him/her. When the sufferer is a priest he/she may consider whether it is appropriate to disclose details; some do and some do not. 'How are you . . . soon becomes by implication, at least in the sick person's ears, "why are you not (yet) better?"'[46] Barbara Baisley found that there were occasions when 'I smile as usual. But inside I'm screaming . . . it took time "to respect myself in weakness".'[47] Anger often follows. Job, through all his vicissitudes, does not curse God: 'Why do you hide your face?' (Job 13.24 NIV); 'My spirit is broken, my days are extinct' (Job 17.1); yet, in his extraordinary faith, he affirms: 'Though he kill me, yet I will trust in him' (Job 13.15). Jesus' cry of dereliction from the cross, 'My God, my God, why have you forsaken me?'(Matthew 27.46; Mark 15.33), so eloquently expresses the aloneness, the doubting in that moment, of the purpose of such excruciating pain. It is a cry which has echoed down the ages, for it encapsulates the problem of pain; the way of the passion becomes part of the Christian disciple's way of life. Suffering does not separate us from God and it is, at times, transfigured 'as a place of encounter with God where we make a gift (sacrifice) and God invites us to . . . himself by bearing the suffering with us'.[48]

A lens through which some have viewed serious and terminal illness is a cycle of grieving, and several authors and contributors have either referred to this overtly or have implied a process with identifiable stages through which they have travelled. Elisabeth Kubler-Ross identified five stages of emotional response in patients with terminal cancer: denial ('it doesn't seem real'), anger ('why me; what have I done to deserve this?'), bargaining – often with God – ('just let me live till my

---

46 Mayne, *A Year Lost and Found*, p. 19.

47 Baisley, *No Easy Answers*, p. 67.

48 Dorothee Soelle, *The Silent Cry: Mysticism and Resistance*, Fortress Press, 2001, p. 138.

daughter's graduation'), depression and, finally, acceptance.[49] Tony Walter suggests that Kubler-Ross's approach may be used by medical staff, family and close friends as a way of avoiding listening to a dying person. 'The stages are a lot neater than the reality of dying for many people . . . (and) her theory does seem particularly prone to criticism for being misused.'[50] Others have added alternative stages: shock, anxiety/fear, desolation, resignation, reconciliation, transformation ('the beauty of the twisted tree is still brought out through its contortion').[51] One of the most profound models is that proposed by Dorothee Soelle, comprising three elements: 1 Apathy (silence and isolation); 2 Articulation (lament, expression and 'psalmic language' in which liturgy plays an important part); 3 Action (change and a deeper sense of unity and completeness with others).[52] And phases may recur: 'Whenever I am faced with a recurrence or a new treatment I go through the same sense of shock and helplessness',[53] as Peter Kerr also describes in Chapter 9.

Some individuals explore 'their most urgent feelings, conflicts (and) yearnings' through ritual, perhaps in the creation of new ritual – which may be very simple.[54] Learning 'how to improvise, how to remain open to the unexpected' requires a journey into the interior in which trials 'or passages of the soul' are to be expected; 'we pass from one state of being into another'. Bernhard Anderson writes of the 'Ritual of Lament' in which the individual: calls out to/addresses God in prayer; complains to God about their concerns and feelings; confesses to trust in God and lists all the ways they are conscious of this in spite of health concerns; appeals to God; seeks to use words

---

49 Elisabeth Kubler-Ross, *On Death and Dying*, Tavistock, 1970.

50 David Kessler, *On Grief and Grieving: Finding Meaning through the Five Stages of Loss*, Simon & Schuster, 2005, quoted in Tony Walter, *The Revival of Death*, Routledge, 1994, pp. 72–3.

51 Spufford, *Celebration*, p. 83.

52 Soelle, *The Silent Cry*, p. 164.

53 Baisley, *No Easy Answers*, p. 14.

54 James Roose-Evans, *Passages of the Soul: Rediscovering the Importance of Rituals in Everyday Life*, Element, 1994, p. xii.

of assurance of certainty that what is asked for will be heard; and assures God of their love.[55] There are many ways in which simple and practical ritual may be involved in the loving care of the sick – the carefully prepared and shared meal, holding a hand, massaging the feet, or the celebration of Communion at the bedside, for example. And those approaching death who are enabled to be conscious of the rite of passage experience an unalterable shift in perception, a *metanoia*, often helped by a quiet loved one or palliative care professional accompanying them.[56] 'What is this fear of dying? Is it not compounded of all our fears? And is it not *fear* which ultimately has to be exorcised by ritual?'[57] 'It is a process brought about not by intellectual debate, but by direct experience.'[58] In their desolation many have lamented in the words of the psalmist:

> Hear my prayer O Lord,
> let my cry come to you
> Do not hide your face from me
> On the day of my distress
> . . . My days are like an evening shadow;
> I wither away like grass (Psalm 102.1–2, 11)

> How long O Lord? Will you forget
> me for ever?
> How long will you hide your face
> from me? (Psalm 13.1)

The theology of the cross and practice of lament are vital in the midst of suffering (see Gordon Mursell's Afterword). Lament

55 Bernard Anderson, *Out of the Depths: The Psalms Speak for Us Today*, Westminster John Knox Press, 2000, pp. 76–7.

56 Marie de Hennezel, 'A French palliative care psychologist', in *Intimate Death*, Time Warner, 1998, describes how she is 'filled with that particular sense of peace that comes over me each time I meditate by the side of someone who has just died', p. 40.

57 de Hennezel, 'A French palliative care psychologist', p. 6.

58 de Hennezel, 'A French palliative care psychologist', p. xiii.

has the potential for enabling patient, family and healthcare providers to be honest and faithful Christians in acknowledging that the God they pray to is alongside the suffering, enabling reconciliation and absorbing the anger and pain. John Hull writes of God 'going beyond compassion to anger on our behalf, and finally by becoming one of us . . . starts by healing us in anger and finishes by participating in our lives though love'.[59] While lament outnumbers other themes in the Psalms, prayers for deliverance – 'I suffered distress and anguish . . . O Lord, I pray, save my life' (Psalm 116. 3–4); and protection – 'You who live in the shadow of the Most High . . . will say to the Lord, "My refuge and my fortress"' (Psalm 91.1) are a source of comfort to the sick.[60] Michael Mayne, in the last weeks of his life, wrote, 'I have sought to keep faith with the Psalmist: "My heart is steadfast, O God, my heart is steadfast; I will sing and make melody"' (Psalm 57.7).[61]

Metaphors and parables occur throughout the Bible as ways of conveying meaning for the indescribable/inexplicable 'mystical sensibility'.[62] And these, in turn, become metaphors for us in seeking ways of conveying meaning in pain and anxiety. Whether they are metaphors to describe creation or parables such as the Prodigal Son or the Good Samaritan, they are ways of leading to knowing through unknowing. Suffering does not separate us from God, although some, in the depths of physical and mental pain, may feel separation. At such times Gethsemane and the cross may express the inexpressible. Suffering may put us in touch with the 'mystery of reality' when words cannot adequately describe the experience; it may be transfigured as a place of encounter with God where the individual makes a gift (sacrifice) and God bears the suffering with him/her. Paul exhorts believers to 'complete what is lacking in

59 John M. Hull, *In the Beginning there was Darkness*, p. 168.

60 Anderson, *Out of the Depths*, pp. 66, 76, 121, 212.

61 Michael Mayne, *The Enduring Melody*, Darton, Longman and Todd, 2006, p. 245.

62 Soelle, *The Silent Cry*, p. 21.

Christ's afflictions' (Colossians 1.24). In their journeys through deep pain and anxiety, some writers, both priests and lay, use metaphor, while others adopt oxymorons, mutually exclusive concepts to explore the paradox of something that is hard to understand and harder to articulate (e.g. 'silent cry', 'sight in the dark', 'filled emptiness'). It is that move towards mystical language, that 'boundary between speech and speechlessness' which is so clearly articulated by Hildegard of Bingen when she wrote of the 'shadow of the living light'.[63] Michael Mayne wrote of feeling upheld in the days leading up to surgery for advanced throat cancer 'but in the dark days that followed I felt nothing at times but the darkness . . . (I) felt the darkness of desolation in the Garden of Gethsemane and, for a while, on the Cross'.[64] For some, words are inadequate; Ben de la Mare echoed Margaret Spufford in finding that music spoke to him more eloquently than words, for music seemed 'to harmonize opposites and state paradox'.[65]

Inner feelings were hidden by some authors: 'Outwardly I was cheerful and stoic; inwardly I was in chaos.'[66] 'No one ever told me that fear felt so like grief! Fear was what dominated me . . . And worse, I was ashamed of my fears . . . I was afraid and I felt that God had betrayed me.'[67] Inga Clendinnen acknowledged, 'Courage was possible in daylight. When night came I had no defence . . . I was frightened.'[68] Gillian Rose, on being told of her advanced ovarian cancer told the specialist, 'I am the happiest, healthiest person I know.' 'Well,' replied the consultant, 'you are going to be very severely tried.' Her unspoken response was, 'I like him for putting it like that. It leaves me be.'[69] During the period of

63 Quoted in Soelle, *The Silent Cry*, p. 72.

64 Mayne, *The Enduring Melody*, p. 81.

65 Spufford, *Celebration*, p. 19.

66 Baisley, *No Easy Answers*, p. 6.

67 Baisley, *No Easy Answers*, p. 14.

68 Inga Clendinnen, *Tiger's Eye: A Memoir*, Jonathan Cape, 2001, p. 18.

69 Gillian Rose, *Love's Work*, Vintage, 1997, p. 77.

shock and anxiety, perhaps before it is clear what treatment is possible or desirable, or when treatment has begun and the prognosis is unclear, a number of priests have written about the difficulty that they had in praying or saying the offices. Some (e.g. Rachel Lewis) have felt sustained by well-loved biblical passages, while others (e.g. Jane Kenchington) have sung hymns. Michael Mayne, when writing of his experience of ME, acknowledged, 'I neither had the will nor the desire to say the offices' and, regarding prayer, 'when you are ill you need others within the Body to do that for you'.[70] Peter Kerr acknowledges this. Was God absent? Ben de la Mare echoes Michael Mayne who said, 'Yes', in that God could not be sensed and, 'No', since others acted as channels of his love.[71] It is, perhaps, in the depths of pain and despair that the 'cloud of forgetting' is a gift of grace. It may enable the sense of freedom by which the individual can sense the 'inner stirring of love in the dusk of the cloud of unknowing'.[72] 'God', writes Trystan Owain Hughes, 'does not offer a supernatural rescue to us, but he does become a supernatural resource for us . . . he serves to strengthen and inspire us as we become more and more aware of his grace.'[73]

Inga Clendinnen suffered severe liver failure and, after more than a year, her situation exacerbated by mis-diagnosis, she waited for a transplant. 'It is not possible to hope, because you know everything depends on chance: the savage chance of a brutal accident somewhere in some not too remote place . . . that a family in the midst of anguish will hear and agree to a barbarous request . . . People on the waiting list are always secretly tense on public holidays. Road accidents happen on public holidays.'[74] Following major surgery the administration of high dosages of pain-relieving morphine took its toll

70 Mayne, *A Year Lost and Found*, pp. 12, 13.

71 Mayne, *The Enduring Melody*, p. 81.

72 Soelle, *The Silent Cry*, p. 58.

73 Trystan Owain Hughes, *Finding Hope and Meaning in Suffering*, SPCK, 2010, p. 99.

74 Clendinnen, *Tiger's Eye*, p. 172.

on some who wrote of hallucinations, 'nothing works . . . feel, for the first time, a real sense of desolation'.[75] Inga Clendinnen had four days of terrifying 'pure malevolence' described with the eye and memory of the literature scholar: 'I do not choose them, they terrify me, I think they will kill me.'[76]

Priests who have come through major illness acknowledge a profound process of transformation:

> when someone says, 'How nice to see you back; are you fully recovered now?' the answer's no: and I won't be. It's not about recovering; it's not about sticking up the cracks, as if the object of the exercise was to get back to where I was before: that's never possible for any of us.[77]

Rachel Lewis, after re-constructive surgery, reflects on this; Christopher Collingwood acknowledges that there is no going back to where he was before; Kevin Ellis writes of how he has come to terms with sterility; Jane Tillier rejoices in her one child.

For some there is a terminal prognosis. Acceptance was marked for Barbara Baisley by 'being worried less about why I had cancer (as she) began to ask instead what I could do with and in this situation'.[78] Moving accounts have been written of journeying from acceptance to transformation: 'I am on a journey and that journey has a goal. At a deeper level than I had imagined, I have found that this pilgrimage with God is what it means to me to be fully alive.' This focus on (and sometimes joy) in the present moment is something that many have come to recognize as a gift and one which not only benefits the sick. Later Barbara Baisley wrote, 'I no longer worry about the where or why of God. If he is,

75 Mayne, *The Enduring Melody*, p. 70.
76 Clendinnen, *Tiger's Eye*, p. 185.
77 David Stancliffe, Chrism Eucharist sermon, 2009.
78 Baisley, *No Easy Answers*, p. 115.

then: please take me home.'[79] Inga Clendinnen, following her successful liver transplant, reflected on her state: 'I am different now, now that I know what I'm made of . . . Just a ragbag of metaphors, a hank of memories, and a habit of interrogation, held together by drugs.'[80] She, together with other transplant, patients 'will remain guinea pigs, experimental animals, for as long as we live or, if you prefer, Angels born on the wings of our drugs, dancing on the pain of mortality'.[81] And beyond this? Barbara Baisley, acknowledging that she had no choice about dying, meditated on the story of Lazarus. She acknowledged that she was still afraid, 'And Jesus sits there and strokes the dog gently on the head then reaches out and takes my hand. "I know," he says. "So am I."'[82] To die 'with gratitude for all that has been, without resentment for what you are going through, and with openness towards the future, that is the greatest gift we can leave to those who love us and who are left behind . . . (we are) summoned to a sense of wonder at nature's *cantus firmus*. A melody that is both hopeful and enduring.'[83] Each of us struggles to describe in images what is happening, sharing a language which is inadequate to describe the 'mystical moments of wholeness' when experience does not represent the objective reality that surrounds us and words are inadequate.[84] Mark Cobb, writing of the contribution of spiritual care in palliative care writes 'we can find in death a glimpse of the sacred which is both awesome and fascinating . . . in approaching death through suffering and sorrow we may find ourselves having to walk on holy ground'.[85]

And who, some authors have mused, should write their story? The answer, Gillian Rose suggests, is everyone; 'It is

79 Baisley, *No Easy Answers*, pp. 187, 197.
80 Clendinnen, *Tiger's Eye*, p. 188.
81 Clendinnen, *Tiger's Eye*, p. 282.
82 Baisley, *No Easy Answers*, p. 47.
83 Mayne, *The Enduring Melody*, p. 251.
84 Soelle, *The Silent Cry*, p. 55.
85 Mark Cobb, *The Dying Soul*, Open University Press, 2010, p. 2.

quite enough, simply, to be a human being, to have something to tell'; there is much to learn 'from entering into another's existence, to touch the subtlest fibres of another's heart and to listen to its beating'.[86] When, having been diagnosed with terminal cancer, Michael Mayne embarked on his last book, he began by addressing the question of whether it was an act of self-indulgence. He suggests that sharing a common human experience can help to authenticate 'perfectly normal valid feelings . . . when we walk in the shadowlands of illness, pain or grief'. And that those who have 'learned to feel their way through different forms of darkness . . . recognize each other and are more likely to turn to those who have been there too. The gift of empathy is all the better for being hard-won.' And each person's experience is unique: 'It is my operation and my cancer: like that of others but just that crucial bit unlike too.'[87] Narrative 'like sacraments, can be signs that do things . . . a story can have a practical and performative (ritual) aspect, not just a descriptive function'.[88] Storytelling, Hopewell reminds us, develops evocation, an awareness 'that we are'; followed by characterization, the deepening sense of 'who we are', and concludes with confession, the acknowledgement of 'what we are'.[89] Each person's story shares features in common with others' but how each person responds in their situation is unique.

We each respond differently to the same piece of music, novel, painting or country walk 'When I am ill, it is my illness, my ME, my cancer, and it takes on my particular characteristics.'[90] And why priests? Dame Cicely Saunders, founder of the hospice movement, spoke of the pain which people with serious illness may experience: physical pain which may be controlled (but not always) by the expert use of modern drugs and

86 Rose, *Love's Work*, p. 112.

87 Mayne, *The Enduring Melody*, pp. xvi, 82.

88 James F. Hopewell, *Congregation: Stories, and Structures*, Fortress Press, 1987, p. 193.

89 Hopewell, *Congregation*, p. 194.

90 Mayne, *The Enduring Melody*, p. 22.

spiritual pain, soul pain, where a person's 'very identity seems to be disintegrating'.[91] We believe that priests have a special role in writing of soul pain and their approach to achieving wholeness; from being in the present to be-coming. It is in this spirit that this book of essays is offered.

91 Quoted in Mayne, *The Enduring Melody*, pp. 33, 34.

2

The Experience of Stroke and the Life of the Spirit

BEN DE LA MARE[92]

There is a personal story of sometimes bewildering complexity behind every stroke. 'But why is stroke any different from other serious illness?' In this chapter I seek to identify some of the distinctive characteristics of strokes; but I leave it to others to answer the question more adequately. It only needs to be stated here that all strokes, in some measure, affect *mental* processes, sometimes profoundly; and we easily underestimate the extent to which our performance is affected by our state of mind.

My brain surgeon was a little surprised when I raised the question of 'spiritual impact'. He had plenty to say about the process of physical recovery; and he was even more interested in stimulating a revival of mental appetite. But he left it there. I took his point; and so I shall attempt here to begin to answer my own question. My training was in theology, which is why I believe that all pastoral ministry within the Christian Church should come under the searching scrutiny of theology. That scrutiny ought to extend to cover the personal experience of the minister.

---

92 Written by the late Ben de la Mare in 2004–05. Ben gratefully acknowledged help and encouragement from Frances Arnold, Frances Dower and above all his wife, Clare Stancliffe, who has given permission for this version of Ben's paper to be published. Reproduced from *Medical Humanities* 31.2, 2005, with permission from the BMJ Publishing Group; and the *Fairacres Chronicle* 2008.

I am not the only stroke patient who hates the intended sympathy of: 'I know just what it feels like.' We survivors have all lived before *and* after stroke. We know very well the effect it has on energy levels, staying power, getting things completed, appetite and zest for life, mood and much else. For some of us, these all culminate in the effect of stroke on faith, prayer, and moral urgency. If our interlocutor has travelled all these by-ways of the human spirit, and others too, then perhaps he or she does know 'what it feels like'.

Almost exactly eight years before the stroke I had become seriously ill; and on that occasion I had to endure two weeks in hospital before the doctors decided that the rigours and a violently fluctuating temperature were being caused by a heart infection (sub-acute bacterial endocarditis or SBE). The illness had already sapped my energy; but after two months I had to face the further blow of not getting better, once the infection had been driven out. At this point, on my first encounter with the cardiologist, I was offered a drastic remedy: open-heart surgery *in a fortnight*, with mitral valve replacement. I can still remember how this decision came to me as welcome relief but to my wife, Clare, as another brutal shock.

In the early stages of this illness, I hadn't much appetite for reading, or for prayer. But, on my first trip to hospital, I took with me a copy of the poems of George Herbert, and I tried to read one poem a day. My instinct must have told me that *he* would best nourish the spirit, when more conventional prayer dries up. When the awesome day of the operation came, with the inevitable two-hour delay, I had arrived at 'Obedience'; and these lines leaped from the page and imprinted themselves on my memory:[93]

> O let thy sacred will
> All thy delight in me fulfill!
> Let me not think an action mine own way,
> But as thy love shall sway,
> Resigning up the rudder to thy skill.

93 C. A. Patrides (ed.), *The English Poems of George Herbert*, J. M. Dent & Sons Ltd, 1974, p. 118.

At that critical juncture, Herbert spoke to me as one who is thoroughly at home in the language of prayer (often in the robust style of the Psalms). Once his words had sunk in, I knew that I must neither seek nor claim any special favours from God. The operation was successful; and after another four months off work, I resumed the full round of my duties, until this second blow struck.

Stroke was something quite new. The phrase 'brain attack' conveys something of the violence of the impact. For it affects everything, especially the decision that has to be made: *should* life go on? During that shadow time when consciousness was allowed to return, I was dimly aware of a choice still to be made: 'to live or not to live'. Was it as simple as that? Perhaps; perhaps not, though I do distinctly remember a period when, to me, extinction really didn't matter. The raw experience of existence was so awful. Even then, however, I could still understand my value to those who are closest to me. This may go some way to explain my reported response to the innocent question: 'What shall I tell them in church tomorrow?' following my restoration to consciousness. I replied: 'Indestructibly hopeful.' I don't remember saying this, but others have said that it's authentic and I'd like to think that those two words brought a smile. They also offer just a hint of a life sometimes disciplined by the study of theology; and with hindsight, I suggest also that the decision not to give up might have been shaped by the words of Jesus beginning: 'not my will/*not what I want, but . . .*' (Luke 22.42).

In those early days of returning awareness and right through my two months in hospital, I seemed to be faced with the withdrawal of God. I have said to friends that 'I was *reduced* to praying, because that was almost the only thing I could gladly do.' That sounds odd, but then the circumstances were strange and unfamiliar; and bodily weakness may have made the mind more alert. I didn't eat for a fortnight. I couldn't read. I was uninterested in the radio, and I even lost my taste for classical music. In spite of my immobility, however, the determination to focus mind and heart together on the task of prayer prevailed. It was a prayer of the utmost simplicity. Often, just a single word repeated. I think that it sought to drain off lingering self-pity and make more room for the love of God. God's felt absence was real enough, but his love was conveyed through the constant care that surrounded me. There is a paradox for tidy thinkers. And now let me add another: over all those weeks of rehabilitation, God's providence was strongly felt, but not his presence.

Stroke comes in many forms and leaves its survivors with very diverse outcomes. It has been stated that, after cancer and heart attacks, stroke is the third commonest killer in this country. What is less well known is that it leaves more people disabled than any other condition. Children suffer strokes, along with a thousand cases a year affecting the under 30s, and some ten thousand a year among those of working age. Strokes are more often caused by blood clots in the brain. But many, like mine, are caused by bleeding in some part of the brain – cerebral haemorrhage. Many are killed outright by stroke, which represents a severe shock to the system: 'It is like being hit over the head with a sledge-hammer.'[94] If the victim survives the stroke, then its lasting effect will largely be determined by the particular part of the brain affected by the trauma. In my case, the bleeding took place in the cerebellum. Some of the effects of strokes cannot be concealed, as when a degree of paralysis brings consequent disabilities and dependence on a wheelchair; the same is true when there is a slurring of speech with facial disfigurement. Even though an erratic sense of balance, which follows a trauma in the cerebellum, will make walking problematic, this is less evident to casual observers. Many other transient or temporary effects may be experienced; and there will often be an unpredictable pattern of recovery, much influenced by the presence, or absence, of willpower.

Stroke recovery brings with it complex, sometimes stormy moods; stroke presents a varied picture, mixing visible and not so visible effects. But patients will be quick to identify important common characteristics: e.g. the loss of feeling or sensation, and tiredness: 'Tiredness becomes a fact of life.'[95] Another characteristic is an often well-concealed anger or frustration.

---

94 Personal comment from my brain surgeon, Peter Crawford, explaining to my wife, Clare, what I had experienced (2002).

95 Rosemary Sassoon, *Understanding Stroke*, Pardoe Blacker Publishing Ltd, 2002, p. 23.

Before we can seriously address my main theme, I need to focus on the experience of recovery from stroke and, initially, this was dominated by physical recovery. Early on, I had to persuade myself to eat – sweet things were a particular problem; and even the familiar cup of tea lost its appeal and had to be drunk in the hope that its charms would return. Throughout the first six months, I battled hard to regain mobility. Once home, my regular visits to the neuro-physiotherapist played a crucial role; before that, equally important, was the help from the hospital physiotherapist. They made sure that the physical structure was put in the way of best functioning. Going for short walks, twice a day to begin with, was more than mere bodily exercise. Stroke patients with potential for improvement thrive on perceptible signs of progress. ('Last week I walked a mile.') Equally, we are wise to fear those who talk knowingly about our impending arrival at a 'plateau'. Both patient and carer have to resist the very idea of a plateau; instead, they must foster the ambition to go on getting better – whatever that means precisely.

My first conscious encounter with the consultant neuro-surgeon marked a critical moment in my recovery. This was four months after the stroke and two months after I was back at home. He was watching me closely, more closely than I realized; and in response to my enthusiasm for walks, the effect of his comment was 'Yes – but! To what end? Where is the mental stimulation?' He had caught me on the raw, and I knew it. So, a whole new field of endeavour opened up before me; and, after another two years, I am more than ever determined to look for new challenges and to discover areas of life with which I can engage effectively. With reduced mobility and limits on energy, thinking and writing play an important role in my daily routine; and often a heavy mood limits the fruitful time, especially for the very physical activity of writing.

After that meeting with the surgeon, I began deliberately to read more demanding books. I tried to make myself write more letters; but I still find this surprisingly difficult, as well as the routine of keeping on top of communications in general. I am shocked that tiredness can provoke the previously unheard, 'Oh, I can't be bothered.' Good things, however, have been achieved during this past year: a lecture on my grandfather, the poet, has been written up.[96] A paper on George Herbert has been revised[97] and, more amazing, I have written and delivered a new paper on Herbert to a conference. So, I begin to realize that each of these bursts of mental toil has offered me targets that I can achieve; and, more importantly, they have given me possible evidence of the life of the Spirit reviving. The testing of *my* spirit was made clearer when, after a year of recovery and rehabilitation, I had to cope with retirement after thirty-seven years spent mainly in parish ministry. For the two months before I retired, I went through the motions, doing only 'light duties', which has to mean 'doing just what you want to do'. Retirement came as a huge relief; but it was not total.

Thanks to the generous attitude of the Principal of my college, an avowed agnostic, I was enabled to continue in part-time chaplaincy among students. This gave me the sense of a continuing pastoral role, just when I had to let go of my established position; and it was a time when reading and writing did not come easily, but sociability was returning. Since then, much has changed in my condition. I am ready now to bring my chaplaincy to an end. This continuing of a small piece of work has also had a part to play in understanding the life of the Spirit. In such a secular institution, it might well be asked: 'Where is God in this set-up?' To me, God has shown himself as the giver of inner freedom. Being *somebody*, and yet in institutional terms rather an unimportant cog, has helped me to keep my eye on God. The unfulfilled potential of the role has strengthened faith, which is never the worse for a sharp dose of self-knowledge.

To return to weighing up the testing that followed retirement. We already owned a house in Durham, but much work needed to be done on it before we could move in. The work on the new house involved both of us in the business of planning and decision. It also entailed complex and rewarding human relations.

---

96 Ben de la Mare, 'Walter de la Mare, A Traveller to the Edge of Things', in *The Walter de a Mare Society Magazine*, 2004.

97 Ben de la Mare, 'Measure and Meaning in George Herbert's "Discipline"', in *The Seventeenth Century*, 21, 2006, pp. 33–44.

If, at this critical juncture, I had not regained the art of being a sociable creature, I would not have been much help. Instead, the urgency of the work to be done, and the need to plan and talk through a variety of different projects drew me in. In this critical hour, I had rediscovered my love and care for buildings, *and* the pleasure of engaging with people, which is also a hard-learned skill; and it is much more than mere sociability. I prefer to say that we are *relational* creatures. Our creativity, our very humanity, thrives on our engagement with others.

This dramatic conclusion to the year of my stroke may seem to focus chiefly on physical testing; but that only tells half the story. For I came to realize that this great upheaval in *my* life, but also in *our* life together, had much to say about the life of the Spirit. An unsought break in my life's pattern did not provoke a spiritual crisis; but it did make me face the reality of change, and gave me glimpses into the meaning of resurrection.

During the long weeks in hospital, it was one thing to have to make myself eat, but I had also to rekindle my appetite for *life*, my zest, my *joie de vivre*. I could, and still can, be very negative. A black period would settle on me like a cloud. I had to work hard on stretching my stamina and staying power; and I needed to mix with other people. I often spoke of my need to rejoin the human race. Later, there were things like not being allowed to drive, which I accepted, reluctantly. I also became aware of a longing to make myself reconnect with God. I know it cannot be done, just like that; and yet something changed. I shall return to the question of the life of the Spirit, and to the ways in which it may be reshaped by the upheaval of a stroke; but, first, we must hear a little more about the practical effects of recovery, and their implications.

Throughout that first year I was busy relearning some very basic skills, like walking and sustained reading, and being sociable. These not so random skills represent three essential strands in the rope that holds our human nature together. The first, walking, concerns the fact that we are *embodied*. In learning again how to move across a room, and then how to reappropriate the practice and the pleasure of walking, we are attending to the most basic needs of our bodies. I am more aware now than I was before the stroke of the necessity to maintain a good level of bodily health. This does not, must not, constitute an end in itself; but after a major trauma, I know all too well how much my physical form and bodily functioning shapes and influences all aspects of being human. The recovered enjoyment of walking represents the complex realities of embodiment.

What then of intellectual activity: of the kind of thinking that might lead me back to writing? In the early months of recovery, the surgeon had helped me to accept that the activity of walking needs to be complemented by the activity of thinking. This humble word covers so much that is common to human experience. I am now much more aware of the physical effort that goes with this apparently non-physical activity. For now it may be enough to say that an interest in ideas has come back, with increasing force. So, as I have been looking for new ways of testing my stamina, I have realized that thinking must lead on to writing. It may be obvious to others but, for stroke cases, trying to find a way back into life, all that goes with thinking, is much more deliberate. 'Do I want to expend energy on *that*?' More than two years on, writing, with all the mental and physical labour it entails, has become a key activity; but it was well over a year and a half before the ability to focus my mind effectively for writing came back.

It can be argued that the best of our notions, that is the fruits of mental activity, benefit from being challenged and even from being proved wrong by others. Where there is no relationality, we are truly disabled. It is like losing a limb, or being paralysed. In the early days of my recovery, random visitors were not made too welcome. They, unwittingly, showed up my need to learn again how to *relate*. I could only gauge its importance from the experience of having to ration my sociability. I can see now that an excuse was available: 'I'm weary.' But, in time, that had to be challenged and then overcome. It is not quite the same as losing your taste for sweet things; and yet, like that, it *can* be relearned. I knew then, and now I know better, how much care was taken in bringing visitors to my bedside. Clergy in hospital can easily be overwhelmed by well-meaning colleagues, but this did not happen to me. On the contrary, some visitors sensed the need to come alongside me in my undiagnosed *spiritual* isolation. It is unlikely that they knew precisely what they were doing for me, but it is as though *they* represented God; and at the time, I will not have been thinking of there being any *spiritual* significance in their presence. This is what makes any talk about 'the life of the Spirit' so difficult to articulate. Nevertheless, while I was going through a real experience of desolation, the reality of God was mediated to me by people. It was chiefly by their presence and by what they did, much less by what they said.

By friends and family, and by many expert carers in the hospitals, I was being made to think anew about the character of God. 'If there is a God, then what is he like?' One part of me seriously doubted whether I could come up with an answer. But another voice would not let me give up; and for this second voice, the clue may have been found in the unshakeable conviction that I was still a *Christian.* I can see now that, as for other thoughtful Christians facing a crisis, it was the person of Christ himself who stood across my path – like the angel who barred the way for Balaam's ass,[98] saying to me: 'I have been here. Don't be afraid of the darkness.'[99] The mysterious alchemy of faith must originate in a stirring of God's love; but still this rediscovery of the importance of relationality – of valuing people and being valued by them, and of being moved by the love of others to return their love – all these very human exchanges offered me a way back to God.

The stroke patient, who is trying to fight back and to join in some of the hurly-burly of so-called normal life, would gain from being aware of those three strands in our human make-up. Most people who are well take them for granted, but we have to work at them. This much applies to all who suffer a stroke, but the further question began to press on me during my apparent recovery and return to sociable life. I seemed to have accepted that *God is.* But this very practical question remained: 'How do I re-connect with God?' For

98 Numbers 22.22–35.

99 'Whoever follows me will never walk in darkness but will have the light of life' (John 8.12).

I had experienced a real severance – loss – emptiness – vacancy. I never forgot the core language, the language of prayer. However, it is one thing to be able to convince (and to comfort) others that I have an answer, and quite another to convince myself.

Three years have passed since my stroke. My immersion in the life of the Spirit is closer now to where it was before the stroke. Habits of thought about God *have* reconnected with earlier knowledge and practice; and yet the actual practice of prayer has moved on. There is more time, and there are fewer pressures; but those gains are balanced by the real loss of energy. Now I know that physical tiredness affects me to the spiritual centre of my being. So, an inner discipline requires that I learn to wait. For God? Not precisely; but I must wait for the gift of prayer. I have known what it is for this gift to seem to be withheld; but now confidence – and with it, faith – grows stronger. I am willing to wait.

In those first weeks, it was reassuring to find that I still knew my way around the spiritual classics. I would welcome the arrival in my head of lines from Mother Julian of Norwich – 'All shall be well and all manner of things shall be well;' or a phrase from *The Cloud of Unknowing* – 'short prayer pierceth heaven'; or just a single, repeated word from St John of the Cross – *nada, nada, nada, nada, nada* ('nothing, nothing, nothing, nothing, nothing'); or even the closing words on the bookmark belonging to St Teresa of Avila – *solo Dios basta* ('God alone suffices').

To my increasing surprise, and delight, this now seems to be where I want to spend my time. The day ought first to make room for my pondering the deep things of God and the real difficulty of living a recognizably Christian life; only then should I direct mind and heart to the world's mess and all its anguish. I am learning to cope with enforced retirement; and in my daily routine, I seldom need to rush around in expense of nervous energy. Instead, more solitude makes me attentive to an insistent inner voice, which asks, 'Are you for God?' And in spite of all my agony of spirit, I hear my prompt reply, 'Yes!'

Out of this story of a life restored, does it make sense for us to try to *locate* the life of the Spirit? Part of my answer has already been given: 'in solitude' and 'as an unsought gift'; and we might fill that out by saying 'in a setting of God's choosing'. For me, however, another answer must also be offered. For, in spite of all its faults, its follies and its failings, the Church must be the first place for me to seek evidence of the life of the Spirit. I have tested the truth of this assertion. Not only can I say with honesty that I still love the Church, but also I understand well that the Church has been good to me. Now, as time goes on, I relish more and more the recovered status of lay Christian; but even this status is qualified, since from time to time, I still enjoy the privilege of presiding at the parish communion. It is a pleasure to be just a part of a praying community again; and I greatly value those around me in a village congregation, where it is evident that Christian love and care, respect and lightness of heart are all at work.

It seems as though, after the stroke, I have been stripped down – could it be to essentials, in regard to the life of the Spirit? Now I am spared most of the burdens of administration. Now, in all my engagement, and disengagement, with or from people, I shall try to give a more complete response to that inner voice. For I want to say in body, in mind and in all relations, not only human: 'Yes to God, in all the mystery of divine being'; 'Yes to Jesus Christ, who is that mystery made visible'; and 'Yes to the Spirit of God, whose energy informs our prayer and shapes all the good in our lives.' And with slowly increasing conviction, despite my diminishment, I try to say, 'Yes to life, in all its unexpectednesses.'

To conclude: I *see* a little less (the bleeding affected the optic nerve); but perhaps I hear more acutely – noticeably the birds. And much that was always striking and beautiful now moves me more: 'A greater intensity?' That sounds good! But when it comes to human suffering and the spoiling of the natural world, I sometimes experience a closing down of emotions. (I referred earlier to a loss of moral urgency.) Or, is that nothing to do with the consequence of stroke?

My long-standing interest in the seventeenth-century poet, George Herbert, seemed to be switched off for at least a year and a half; and then it came back to life. He has a phrase for every twist and turn of life: 'In age I bud again.'[100] Herbert is the master of metaphor and of the anatomy of the spiritual life; and he prompts me to make an ending with the suggestion that the life of the Spirit is a great river. It flows on with a strong current. It carries us in a certain direction, but it does not depend upon me or you. It speaks to us of the strength and the continuity of God's love for us, and for all that he has made. We may find it harder to accept that the stirring of the Spirit brings disturbance into our lives; and that includes the disturbance of death. But, in my experience, the Spirit of God takes away fear, and replaces it with love. And that I now know to be true, with a knowledge wrung from the experience of faith.

100 'The Flower', *The English Poems of George Herbert*, p. 172.

3

An Affair of the Heart

BRIAN ANDREWS

O vast tranquil peace,
so profound in the gloaming.
How weary are we of wandering –
Is this, perhaps, death?[101]

The last stanza of the Joseph von Eichendorff's poem, 'Im Abendrot' ('At the gloaming') describes the experience of some as they die. For many, death is sudden when, as far as we know, they have no time to think or register what is happening. For others, it is violent, shot through with terror or excruciating pain and, for yet others, it is lingering and painful. But for me, as I lay dying in April 2009, there was no pain and no fear, only a vast, tranquil peace as the components of my body began to shut down.

The medical technology which was attached to me, but of which I was hardly aware, recorded the facts: that my blood pressure was so low that a device to measure it had to be brought from the intensive care unit of the hospital as I couldn't be moved there. My heart rate was very high and irregular, and my heart muscle was getting weaker. I was suffering from cardiomyopathy (disease of the heart muscle) and ventricular tachycardia. However forceful the contractions of the heart, it never empties all the blood out of the ventricle. The normal function of what is called ventricular ejection is 55%–70%.

101 'Im Abentrot', a poem by Joseph von Eichendorff (1788–1857), set to music in 1948 by Richard Strauss as the last of his 'Four Last Songs'.

Under 35% is life threatening. In April 2009 mine was 22%. I was dying.

I shall sketch briefly the events leading to this state of affairs. In my youth and at university I had been a competent middle distance runner. I had rowed, played soccer and rugby and, up to the age of fifty, I had run a few half marathons.

My father died of cardiomyopathy at the age of fifty-six. Two of his brothers died at a similar age from heart-related illnesses and I began to worry about the condition of my own heart. I had psychosomatic symptoms which continued for several years. A patient Christian GP in Hertfordshire reassured me, year after year, and showed, with successive tests, that my heart was in good condition. Gradually I came to believe it. Early in 1998 in my sixtieth year, however, my heart rhythms were sufficiently abnormal for me to be investigated by a cardiologist. The diagnosis was mild cardiomyopathy which was either familial or caused by earlier viral infection. I also had abnormal rhythms from both the ventricle and the atrium. All of this was very successfully suppressed by drug treatment. Ten years later, just before my seventieth birthday, I became increasingly breathless and began to find walking difficult. The rhythms became increasingly abnormal and the tachycardia increased. A GP referred me to a cardiologist whom I visited on Maundy Thursday and he agreed to do an echocardiogram the following day even though there would not be other staff available on Good Friday.

We discussed the implantation of a cardioverter defibrillator, of which more later, after having an MRI scan in Oxford. But a further deterioration made the latter impossible. Eight days after Easter I was admitted to hospital in Gloucester and the events outlined at the beginning of this chapter took over.

For two days I remember little. The cardiologist was contacted at Kingsholm, while watching Gloucester play rugby, and came to the hospital after the game. He stayed for three hours. He advised my wife, Irene, to stay and the ward arranged for her to have an adjacent room where she could sleep and where she stayed, on and off, for a fortnight. Our three adult children were sent for, but I was hardly aware of them. I was not expected to last the night. I did, however, do so, but on Thursday there was another relapse and the expectation was that I would not see the morning.

Dying

It was, for me, an almost painless process. I had very little awareness of, or interest in, anything or anyone. I was aware of the family being present and I was grateful for that, but I was hardly able to communicate with them. My one need was for Irene to stay with me. This she did heroically and out of deep love. She snatched a few hours sleep but came whenever I asked for her. One of my few memories is of a daughter-in-law who was five months pregnant. She was forty-one years old and had suffered many miscarriages. My hand was placed on her abdomen as it was thought that this was as close as I would ever get to see the child as yet unborn.

The image I have is of a dark tunnel with the aperture becoming narrower. It was a peaceful place with little or no awareness of anything else. I was almost overwhelmingly weary. I was content to be; I had little ability to do anything else. I was aware of God. I do not think I prayed for healing; that was too cerebral. But I silently praised and worshipped him, very quietly in my mind and quite undramatically. This always has been, and still is, my most natural prayer. What energy there was in my mind was God and, at a conscious level, the nurturing that I was given by Irene, the medical staff and my family.

Verses from the psalms ran through my head, time and time again. Not the recital of complete psalms or long passages, but a verse or verses which repeatedly came into my mind. The Sanctus, the Jesus Prayer: this was my inner language. I was not afraid; I was beyond caring. It may be that many people, in such a situation, use or revert to, the kind of praying to which they are accustomed because they do not have the energy to do anything else.

Physically, I am told, I rallied on Wednesday but Thursday brought a second crisis. Later I was told that our older son, Nicolas, telephoned my sister Sarah in Dorset and told her, on medical information, that I had only a couple of hours to live. Sarah and her husband Joe were both medical professionals. They immediately drove to Gloucester. During their journey Nicolas phoned them to say I had rallied again.

It was in the early hours of Friday morning, three days after my admittance to hospital, that I told Irene that I thought I would pull through. Clearly I had been aware that I was very ill but I remember no more than that. In the middle of May, twenty-five days after being admitted, I was discharged from hospital.

The immediate aftermath

A nurse from the Gloucestershire Heart Failure service visited me daily for nearly four weeks and then weekly for three months. I had monthly appointments with the cardiologist which the following year were put on a quarterly basis. This arrangement continues.

Ten days after my time in hospital I had the postponed MRI scan in Oxford.

Three weeks later in Gloucester an ICD was implanted. This is a remarkable device similar to a pacemaker. But whereas a pacemaker emits electrical impulses to stimulate the heart to contract and does not give an electric shock, an ICD (implantable cardiovioverter defibrillator) also gives a light shock to restore the heart to a normal rhythm (cardioversion). If this doesn't work, or if there is serious rhythm disturbance, the ICD gives a bigger shock (defibrillation) to stop the abnormal beating and gets the heart rhythm back to normal. The device, a pulse generator, is slightly larger than a small matchbox and weighs three ounces. It is inserted below the collar bone and electrode leads link it with the heart. The ICD records every heart movement and it is possible to read it, electronically, to ascertain the time, date and seriousness of any disturbance. This continues to be done every three months.

Most people, among whom I am one, feel positive after an ICD implant. It is reassuring to know that you cannot now die suddenly from a heart attack. The defibrillator will kick in. It is, literally, a life saver. But it is an invasive process and some people feel uncomfortable about having a foreign body implanted. Which is where the North Gloucestershire ICD Support and Information came in. The group, and especially the two men who drew it together, provided psychological support and practical information and advice. The group has also been proactive in raising money to provide an automated external defibrillator in a sports centre for those suffering sudden cardiac arrest. Although the group is no longer active, because of the death through cancer of one of its two guiding lights, it has provided help and support for many people and their partners in the county.

The healing process

I was in a cardiology unit and treated by two cardiologists who were outstanding. It seems to me that the efficiency of a hospital ward and its care of patients depends on the leadership of the senior staff who run it. There are instances of bad practice, poor nursing and insensitive caring in some hospitals. I have seen this over the years as a parish priest. There are patients who contract infection in hospitals and whose health and well being declines rather than improves. There is aural evidence and substantiated proof for all this throughout the country both in NHS and private hospitals. The care and skill shown to me was of the highest quality. The staff communicated with each other at all levels; patients mattered to them. This was fundamental to my recovery.

The sacraments of the Church and the prayers of individuals and congregations, and the goodwill of those without any religious faith, were essential to me. A colleague anointed me early in the process and the chaplaincy staff visited, prayed with me and administered Holy Communion. Another colleague laid hands on me. As well as its therapeutic effect, it was a learning experience for me even after forty-five years of ordained ministry. He did so when Irene, our three adult children and their married partners were with me, and all laid hands on me. This was a powerful and emotional experience for them and for me which happened four days after my admission.

I have often heard people say how they had felt upheld by the prayers of other people. That was my experience. To know that congregations in the churches where I now live, in the parish from which I had retired four years previously, and in two cathedrals, as well as other individuals, were praying for me was subjectively uplifting and was, I think, used by God towards my healing. As I grew stronger I said the daily Office.

I had an exceptional amount of post, which perplexed the hospital staff, and I had visits from local friends.

I have a loving and caring family who put up with considerable inconvenience and disruption in the lives of their own families to be with me. The parents of a second daughter-in-law flew from Ireland almost at a moment's notice to look after the children of the family. One of the most poignant moments was when a son in his early forties leaned over to me to say goodbye, shed tears onto my face and said: 'Fight, Daddy, fight', a term he had not used for nearly forty years.

Irene, as I have already said, cared for me heroically and out of deep love. She is a highly intelligent, strong and sensitive woman whose willingness and ability to care for me seemed infinite. I may have mattered to her but she mattered to me with a closeness which perhaps exceeded anything we had known throughout our marriage. Our daughter Elizabeth, built of similar stuff, supported and cared for her and stayed with me while Irene slept. Physically, my greatest therapy was to have my legs and feet massaged – something which they seemed to do for hours on end. The boys were no less supportive of Irene, and intelligent and caring in their support of me. They worked as a team, though I hardly knew a half of it.

The cardiologists pored over the printouts of different machines. They thought and talked together. It was possible, metaphorically, to see their brains working. Theirs was not a standard response to, for them, a not uncommon situation. They treated my illness as a new experience with new variables and they changed and re-changed the medication.

Nine months later I was impressed by the humility shown in a letter I received from one of them: 'quite why or how your heart function has improved to such a degree is unclear. It would obviously be helped by the medication you are taking, but that can only explain a small part of the improvement. Nevertheless, this makes your prospects very good . . .' Initially his prognosis was a year; later this was changed to five or more. Lightheartedly he said, 'I suppose you'll think this has something to do with God.' 'Prayer and Co Enzyme Q10,' I replied. CoEnzyme Q10 is a supplement which helps to support cardiovascular health. We owe this information to the daughter of a neighbour who is a qualified nurse and who now practises 'alternative' therapies.

Recently, both specialists said independently that I was a miracle. That is clearly hugely encouraging. But what is a miracle? Something which cannot be fully explained by human argument. I would echo the statement of the blind man in John 9.19–26. The Jews asked his parents: 'Is this your son, who you say was born blind? How then does he now see?' His parents answered, 'We know that this is our son, and that he was born blind; but we do not know how it is that he now sees. Ask him; he is of age . . .' To which the man replied: 'One thing I do know, that though I was blind, now I see.'

Healing is a combination of factors. Medication, love and care, skill, prayer and sacraments are intertwined. For a Christian they all come, directly or indirectly from God. An argument with someone who does not share that Christian faith is pointless. All I can say is: 'One thing I do know, that though my heart function was poor, now it has improved to an unexpected degree.' And I thank God for that.

Pain

Not all has been sweetness and light, whatever the present outcome. The machinery which was attached to me, the oxygen mask and the apparently endless injections were tiresome and inconvenient. But they were not a serious problem.

The first significant pain was caused by constipation. This is never pleasant but to go six days without a bowel movement is, at times, excruciating. I had eaten and digested very little in this time but it was, nevertheless, a real problem. Nothing worked to alleviate it. When finally there was relief, I literally shouted with joy. Fortunately I was not on the open ward, but in the lavatory where, still wired up, I had been taken.

Then there was an attempt at a catheter ablation. This involves a catheter or tube being inserted in the groin and guided up a vein to the heart where it sends electrical impulses to correct an arrhythmia. This is not usually a problem, but for reasons which I don't understand it couldn't be achieved in me and it caused considerable pain.

Sleeping at night became a problem. Few people sleep well in hospital but, even armed with ear plugs and an eye mask, I had increasing difficulty. After the initial improvement in my health I became less tired because I was inactive all day. I needed five pillows to help drain my lungs and I was attached to various gadgetry which severely restricted my movements. I have never been good at coping with a lack of sleep. The importance of a 'good night's sleep' was instilled into me at a very young age and I have found it difficult to re-programme myself. I became very stressed. Eventually this was partly alleviated by mild medication which I used for several months after leaving hospital. There were side effects from some of the medication. This was hardly surprising. One tiresome effect was taste disturbance. I no longer wanted some of the food which previously I had enjoyed eating, and other food, not always the most nutritional, I developed strong longings for. So the medication was adjusted and readjusted. None of these physical or psychological issues compared with the mental suffering which came when I had returned home.

To begin with, I was buoyed up with the joy and wonder of the healing process. God had been good to me and I was grateful. People were welcoming, interested and glad. My physical strength gradually grew. But soon I had a lot of guilt. I felt I should be thankful to be alive; and indeed, in a way I was. Yet increasingly I did not feel thankful or grateful; I became depressed.

I was very pleased that I was able to go by myself to an Old Boys' reunion at my school in Dulwich. I went by coach and bus because I was prohibited from driving for nine months after the ICD implantation. This was an achievement. I was stimulated by it. Irene and I celebrated our forty-fifth wedding anniversary and, belatedly, my seventieth birthday. We had a couple of short holidays and ten days with some of the family in France. Here things began to take a downward turn. It was too soon to have gone abroad and I couldn't cope easily with the heat.

I missed singing at the Three Choirs Festival in Hereford, I didn't feel confident enough to take a wedding in Hertfordshire which had been booked for many months, and I withdrew from a Retreat I was to have led in August. The grandson whom I might never have seen was born in London, but it was exhausting for me to be there.

I began to sing again with the Gloucester Choral Society in September but I lacked confidence and I failed the triennial audition for the Three Choirs. It was seven months before I could celebrate the Eucharist. It was difficult to be alone. When Irene returned to painting classes in the autumn, I was very anxious about being alone even for a few hours. That same month I saw a therapist who reckoned I was one point, on her scale, above being clinically depressed. I had three sessions but found I didn't relate well to her. So that was brought to a close.

It seemed to be a long haul. Physically the improvement continued, but mentally it was so all-pervading. Returning to the hospital for monthly checks restimulated the experience of April, even though I had nothing but praise and thanks for the staff. I was better, but I didn't feel as full of the joys of spring as I thought I should be. Hadn't God brought me up 'out of the pit'? Yes, I knew that he had; it just didn't feel like it. And so my sense of guilt remained and, at times, I wished I had never come through the illness and that my heart had failed totally and comprehensively.

The support and love from Irene continued unabated and gradually the tide began to turn. I began to enjoy my monthly preaching commitment again. Gradually the weight of depression began to lift – or to be lifted – and God's second healing began to bear fruit. After nearly three years, that pain has receded and Irene and I have begun a different experience together.

It was the spring of 2010 before the DVLA would allow me to drive again. Irene had taken me everywhere so it was a good experience and good for my confidence, to be able to drive again and alone. However, we have both reached a period in our lives when we want, less and less, to travel far. We prefer to be at home rather than away, though visiting and spending time with family and friends is something we enjoy most. This, I know, is experienced by many people of our age.

I still suffer from physical tiredness. This might be a result of malfunctioning thyroid glands. It might be partly psychological. It is certainly true that my heart function is still impaired. But the reality also is that, with new medication, I can now walk for two miles on the flat. But an hour's sleep each day with no detrimental effect to the quality of sleep at night, remains a constant factor of life and one which we have learned to live with. Heart failure is a result of damage to the muscles of the heart. This can never be completely healed, even though in my case the muscles have become stronger.

Seasons of the heart[102]

I have become increasingly aware of the heart and its seasons. It is an ancient concept. The heart has long been used as a symbol to refer to the spiritual, emotional, moral and, in the

---

102 The title of a book of haiku poems. Alan Spence, *Seasons of the Heart*, Canongate Books, 2000, also title of a song by John Denver (1943–97).

past, intellectual core of a human being. Aristotle considered the heart to be the seat of thought, reason and emotion. In Egyptian mythology, the heart was weighed against a feather in the judgement of the dead.

In the Bible the word 'heart' is almost never used literally, an exception being the reference to the 'breastpiece . . . on Aaron's heart' (Exodus 28.30); rather, it is used metaphorically, as today in common parlance. It was often used to mean commitment to a cause as when, for example, the people of Israel entered into a covenant to 'seek the Lord . . . with all their heart and with all their soul' (2 Chronicles 15.12); 'happy are those who keep his decrees, who seek him with their whole heart' (Psalm 119.2). But 'the heart is devious above all else; it is perverse – who can understand it? I the Lord test the mind and search the heart' (Jeremiah 17.9–10).The word was used to embody emotions when the wickedness of humankind grieved God 'to his heart' (Genesis 6.6). The heart is the locus of the affections: 'You shall love the Lord your God with all your heart' (Deuteronomy 6.5). It is also the seat of the intellect: 'every inclination of the thoughts of their hearts' (Genesis 6.5), and the Psalmist 'treasure(s) your word in my heart' (Psalm 119.11). Job was to 'receive instruction from his mouth and lay up his words in your heart' (Job 22.22). While 'anxiety weighs down the human heart' (Proverbs 12.25), the heart is also the source of bravery: 'Let no one's heart fail because of him (Goliath)' (1 Samuel 17.32). The heart signifies humankind's innermost being, e.g. 'his heart was filled with pain' (Genesis 6.6) and Mary, after the visit of the shepherds to the stable, 'treasured all these words and pondered them in her heart' (Luke 2.19). Some of the most evocative references to the heart occur in the Psalms when the psalmist cries out to the Lord in lament: 'my heart is pierced within me' (Psalm 109.22), 'with my whole heart I cry; answer me O Lord' (Psalm 119.145).

It seemed to me that as well as using the word 'heart' in a metaphorical sense, there might be a link between the heart and the brain. My physical heart had become impaired. Might there not be a connection between that and my feelings? It is, of course, obvious that there is a link. Electrical impulses in the body caused by any pain or injury are registered in the mind and the emotions. Similarly any kind of healing results in a positive attitude. We speak of 'getting worse' or 'getting better'. These states register on a scale of positive to negative feeling. But does damage to the heart register in a different way from damage to the lung or leg?

Psychologists once maintained that emotions were purely mental expressions generated by the brain alone. We now know that this is not true: emotions have as much to do with the heart and body as they do with the brain. In 1991 the Institute of HeartMath was established by Doc Childre and Howard Martin in California. This is a research centre dedicated to the study of the heart and the physiology of emotions. The heart is in a constant two-way dialogue with the brain, but the heart sends more information to the brain than the brain sends to the heart. Erratic heart patterns block our ability to think clearly. If this is true, and it seems probable that it is, a damaged heart or one with damaged muscles will be less effective in its communication with the brain and the brain will send out negative or stressful feelings. The rhythms or seasons of the heart are indicative of cardiovascular efficiency and nervous system balance.

The current state of affairs

I have indicated my physical and psychological improvement. I believe this to be the work of God, mediated through medicine, people and through direct influence: the power of God within.

Increasingly, I expect to live longer, certainly longer than early prognoses. Although writing this chapter has caused restimulation of the events of 2009 and I think it not surprising that it has, that period and its effects are gradually receding in my mind. I am still easily tired and I cannot do some physical tasks which previously I could. I haven't recovered my former self-confidence. Perhaps I never shall. And I find it more stressful than before to cope with large groups of people in a confined space.

I am, however, more content with the present and I have less striving for the future. I don't have ambitions, though I still look forward greatly to events. I delight in our six grandchildren in the changing phases of their lives. There are times when my eyes light up at the possibility of a new choral experience or of holidays which we might take. But I don't much mind if they don't happen.

I am content, more so, perhaps, than I have ever been. As far as I am aware, I have no fear of death nor even of dying. Every year is a bonus. God is ever present, and although there are many weaknesses in my thinking and behaving, I think I am ready to, what is often called, 'meet my maker'. I echo a prayer of Alcuin of York, an eighth-century poet, liturgist and Abbot of Tours:

> . . . that with all our heart and mind and soul and strength, we may seek your face and be brought by your infinite mercy into your holy presence.

4

Magnificat

JANE TILLIER

Between 1997 and 2008 we lost nine babies in seven early miscarriages. For most of this time I was a parish priest, well known in the local community. The most common question that I heard went something like, 'How can you still do your job/believe in God/have faith after all that you have been through?' The worst time was when I was flat on my back on a trolley waiting to go in to the operating theatre for yet another 'evacuation of the retained products of conception'. The theatre nurse, checking my notes, saw that my address was 'The Vicarage' and it led her to quiz me on how on earth I could go on believing in God. I felt the need to respond to her not just from the deep-seated place of screaming pain and loss that I was experiencing but also from my role as a public representative of a faith that (at its best) is able to 'hold' the mystery of suffering for people through, in part, the story of a crucified saviour.

One theological perspective on the nature of ordained ministry, found at its most fully developed in the Orthodox tradition, suggests that the priest stands within the Christian community as an εἰκών Χριστου. A suffering minister is still an 'icon of Christ'. Indeed one could argue that this image is even more true to the reality of Jesus; but it can be hard for people to accept and feel comfortable with their priest's pain or loss or grief. It may be that this is particularly the case in contemporary culture where there is a prevailing emphasis on success in all areas of life.

As I was reflecting on this, I came across a short talk by Richard Rohr. As I listened, I smiled at the serendipitous synchronicity of hearing Rohr lament that the Church has so often failed to embrace Jesus as 'an icon of vulnerability'. He attributes all sorts of the world's ills to this failure.[103] Janet Morley reflected on the fact that, in the response to her book, *All Desires Known*, there was almost as much interest in the one collect that addressed the Almighty as 'vulnerable God' as there was in the groundbreaking use of inclusive language and feminine imagery throughout the book.[104] This is not the place to trace the debate around 'patripassianism' (the heretical belief that the Father suffered with the Son). Suffice to say that Christians have long struggled with the extent to which suffering and vulnerability (so fundamental to human reality) are taken in to the heart of the godhead in Christ.[105]

I was very 'public' about my loss and grief. I did not invent a bout of flu to explain my absence from parish duties for a few days each time I miscarried. This is probably mostly due to the fact that I am a raging extrovert and so it is difficult for me to keep my realities hidden. But, on a more positive note, I also saw the pastoral fruits of shared experience in all sorts of ways. Miscarriage is far more common than many people realize. Something like one in three confirmed pregnancies end up not being viable. Parishioners spoke tenderly to me of their own times of pregnancy loss. Some were very elderly and yet it was the first time they had shared their story in any depth. Tears were shed. Prayers were offered. And my sense was that people found a measure of healing in these encounters.

In a similar vein, I wrote once in a 'Vicar's letter' in the monthly parish magazine of my experiences of paralysing depression. I tried to explain the way in which I had had to lean on the prayers of

---

103 Richard Rohr's 'Wish for the world' on YouTube – www.youtube.com/watch?v=dA-KvS4BlLY. I am grateful to Ian Atherton, Jane Besly, John Hegarty, Jeff Leonardi, Chris Rowland and Jennifer Tann for their support and encouragement as I wrote this chapter.

104 In the 1980s I was part of the Women in Theology 'Publications Group' which helped bring to birth the first edition of Janet Morley's *All Desires Known*, Movement for the Ordination of Women and Women in Theology, 1988. This was the soft, small, green version, not the later expanded SPCK version with the striking Georgia O'Keefe cover (1992).

105 The term 'Patripassianism' is given to the modalist heresy which emphasizes the unity of the Trinity at the expense of the plurality: Alan Richardson and John Bowden (eds), *A New Dictionary of Theology*, (Patripassianism, p. 431), (Modalism, p. 375), SCM Press, 1983.

others and I mentioned the solace that I had found in some of the Psalms. In twenty years of writing for parish magazines I have never had as much response as I had to that one letter. People rang me, stopped me in the street to speak to me and sent notes of appreciation for having written about depression, a subject that touched so many of their lives so profoundly, either directly or indirectly, and yet which is so often regarded as a taboo. It mattered to people that, among other things, they could see that I was a woman of sorrows, and acquainted with grief (Isaiah 53.3)

Our honesty about pregnancy loss allowed family, friends, colleagues and parishioners to support us with much love and prayer. It also allowed for a great communal sense of joy when our daughter, Clare, was born in 2000. The announcement that the vicar had had a baby girl was made at the annual 'Old Folk's Treat'. One of our GPs (who, together with the local midwife, had been enormously supportive) went straight from the pensioners' tea party in the village school to the off licence to buy champagne, which he immediately brought to the hospital. And our local post lady laughed with us day by day as she delivered the 367 cards that arrived at the Vicarage to greet Clare's birth.

After our first miscarriage, we received a postcard from our area Bishop offering sympathy and assuring us of prayer. He wrote of the fact that he and his wife had experience of stillbirth. The picture on the card was of his pectoral cross, which had been specially commissioned when he was consecrated. Inscribed on it are the words, 'The weakness of God' (1 Corinthians 1.25). We felt held and understood.

The second miscarriage was medically more complex. Investigations revealed that I had been carrying a 'molar pregnancy'. Something goes wrong in the very early stages of conception and the placenta quickly outgrows the foetus. In 10%–15% of cases this leads to the growth of a 'trophoblastic tumour' which needs chemotherapy treatment. Because of this risk I had to undergo careful monitoring of blood and urine samples for many months and we were advised not to try for another pregnancy for at least a year. I rang my area Bishop's office to ask if he would please be as a parish priest to me. I asked for prayers for healing. I have a vivid memory of kneeling in the little chapel in his house, weeping, and receiving the laying on of hands and anointing. Mercifully I did not develop cancer. Through a mix-up over the delivery of the little boxes from the hospital consultant in Sheffield, to whom I had to post the urine samples, I met a parishioner who did. Her box was mistakenly delivered to me and I took it round to her address. She invited me in for coffee and we shared our stories. She already had a little boy aged three or four. Her head was covered with a scarf and she spoke of the ravages of chemotherapy. Thankfully she made a full recovery and, I discovered when I met her at a party years later, went on to have a second child.

Once every two years all the clergy from our diocese go away to Swanwick for a residential conference. That was the context in which I discovered that my third pregnancy was failing. Just before one of the big services, I discovered that I had started to bleed. As I emerged into the corridor, shocked and distressed, the first person that I saw was Bishop Christopher, who had prayed for me after the last miscarriage. He virtually carried me back to my room and sent someone to fetch one of my friends so that she could drive me home. I remember shouting at him through my tears, 'It's not fair! I really, really thought that it would be alright this time . . .'

People have asked why we went on trying. It is difficult to give an answer. Except to say that each time I became pregnant I had a powerful sense that this time it would go to full term. My final pregnancy (in 2008) came as a complete surprise. We were not 'trying' and I was just about to start a new job. I realized I was pregnant again while I was away with my Clergy Cell Group at my old theological college for twenty-four hours. As I arrived home and prepared to share the news with my husband, I saw an enormous rainbow over our house. It felt like an unequivocal divine affirmation of my hope that this was to be a wonderful, unplanned, 'un-looked for' gift. The tears that I wept three or four weeks later in my hospital bed as it became clear that this pregnancy too was 'not viable' included tears of anger and frustration at a God who seemed to promise so much only to snatch it away when I was least expecting it.

My personal sense of the powerful triumph of hope over experience through these years helpfully informed my ministry when I served as Chaplaincy Team Leader at the local hospice from 2004 to 2008. It was a pattern I saw over and over again in the lives of patients and those close to them. Patients know when they are close to death and yet they, often echoed by their loved ones, say unrealistically optimistic things. In most cases I knew from other honest conversations with them that this was not some form of 'denial'; rather it was a profound human hope that even in the worst of circumstances things can always get better. In the world of palliative care, every small triumph is celebrated and every small positive step encouraged, even in the face of a realistic assessment of imminent death.

Christianity places a great deal of emphasis on hope. My hopes have kept being dashed. Somehow, in a way that is hard to articulate and yet is fundamental to what Jesus offers us, Christian hope is bigger than this sort of frustration; it can encompass profound disappointment, loss and suffering. A vivid picture of that tension is offered when Jesus appears to the disciples after the resurrection and speaks of peace (John 20.19).The Gospel writer notes the continuing presence of the wounds. Woundedness and pain are never fully erased – even by the resurrection – but they are gathered up, incorporated and redeemed.

Some years ago I undertook to work through the Ignatian Spiritual Exercises 'in daily life', using 'the nineteenth annotation'. It was something that I had wanted to do for decades. I find Ignatian spirituality somehow deeply uncongenial (I find it almost impossible to 'enter' imaginatively into a scriptural passage), and yet it has always been profoundly rich in facilitating insight and wisdom for me. I learned much about it from an IBVM nun and have returned to it over and over again throughout my life and I have repeatedly found new moments of, often rather uncomfortable, disclosure under God. In January 2008 I was coming towards the end of the Exercises and was looking at the resurrection narrative in chapter 20 of John's Gospel. I was profoundly struck by what it meant to 'breathe' on someone and this prompted me to write the following:

Gentle as breath

Jesus breathed on them and said to them, 'Receive the Holy Spirit.'
(John 20.22)

Close up,
  intimate:
  the warmth of a lover's breath.

Holy,
  un-looked for:
  the gift of an unseen force.

Wounded,
  peace-bearing:
  the touch of a knowing God.

Jesus,
  gentle as breath:
  the brush of a butterfly's wing.

My experiences of God, of Jesus, of the Holy Spirit have generally been 'gentle' rather than dramatic. I have known God's presence in the touch of friends and family and in the prayers of the community. After one of our early miscarriages I remember sitting on the rug in front of the fire in our sitting room with an old friend who wept with us and sat in silence for a long while before gently articulating a prayer. I was put in mind of the book of Job. Not the pages of words of 'comfort', but the initial reaction of Job's friends, which is described so sparingly at the end of the second chapter: 'They sat with [Job] on the ground for seven days and seven nights, and no one spoke a word to him, for they saw that his suffering was very great' (Job 2.13). In a subsequent reflection, addressing God, I wrote:

Your touch was so soft and tender
we hardly knew you were there.
You sat on the ground with us while we wept.[106]

Shortly after my last miscarriage in July 2008 a dear friend and neighbour, another Jane (who had sat and wept with me on the bed after I came out of hospital), found out that she was pregnant. Some time later she asked if I would be prepared to be her 'birth partner' when she went into labour with this, their fourth, child. The request was offered as a gentle, loving gift. I received it as such. But it catapulted me into another wave of grief over the fact that I had not been able to have more children. What does one do when asked to revisit, in such a tangible way, an area of deep personal woundedness? I found myself reflecting again on an image that I had often used in sermons and talks. In the children's book, *We're Going on a Bear Hunt*, a family sets out with hope: 'We're going on a bear hunt. We're going to catch a big one. What a beautiful day! We're not scared.'[107] Along the way they encounter a variety of obstacles. Each time there is a steady refrain: 'We can't go over it. We can't go under it. Oh no! We've got to go through it!' This seems to me to be an image of what it means as a Christian to 'walk in the way of the cross'. Suffering? Pain? Loss? We can't go over it. We can't go under it. We can't go round it. We've got to go through it . . .[108]

---

106 'Costly Creativity', in *Voices of this Calling*, Christina Rees (ed.), Canterbury Press, 2002, p. 113. The friend was Janet Morley who had written of the 'vulnerable God' in *All Desires Known*. She is one of our daughter's godparents.

107 Michael Rosen, illustrated by Helen Oxenbury, *We're Going on a Bear Hunt*, Walker Books, 1989.

108 As an aside, the conclusion of the bear hunt book is that they find a bear and are so scared that they dash home back through all the obstacles and then, from the safety of the bed covers, they exclaim: 'We're not going on a bear hunt again.' I am not going to let the ending spoil the moral that I draw from the earlier refrain. Another perspective on all this is also added by the fact that when our daughter was little we had to play out this story endlessly whenever we went for a walk.

And so I decided to go 'through' it, to agree to my friend's request. It was hard. But I had the most wonderful, unforgettable experience of journeying with her from when she went into hospital after her waters broke through to the point where her beautiful daughter, Sarika, was resting safely in her arms.

A particularly challenging question for us, in view of my pregnancy history, is that of when one can speak of a 'baby' that has been conceived. Each of ours had a nickname almost as soon as we had a positive pregnancy test. We felt that we could love and talk to whatever/whomever was in my belly from a very early stage. However briefly, I carried ten loved beings in my womb: BAT, MIM, Windy, Popsy, Chrissy, Nevey, Roxy 1, 2 and 3, and finally Pip. The names all have a meaning for us. Roxy 1, 2 and 3 were naturally conceived triplets. It was a big shock at the scan when we were quizzed about whether or not we had been on any fertility treatment (we had not) as we saw three little kidney-bean shapes on the screen. Popsy ('Pregnancy by Ovulation Prediction') was the one who survived to become our much-loved Clare. We loved them all from the beginning. Early scans mean being able to watch the surprisingly fast little heartbeat of the new life growing within. This compounds the sense of loss when it is clear, on a later scan, that there is no longer a heartbeat. It would have been dreadful to have hedged our bets and not to have loved, in those early months, someone who went on to survive.

Pip was about the size of an apple pip when we were explaining about that pregnancy to Clare, who was eight at the time. Much to the occasional surprise of school teachers and others, Clare speaks comfortably of having nine brothers and sisters in heaven. We would have loved to have provided her with a sibling or two. It is part of her story to know that this has not been physically possible. Throughout her years at primary school in a class of nearly thirty children she was the only one who was an only child.

We played it on beaches, in woods, at National Trust properties, and in all sorts of other places. In Clare's version the bear that was chasing us home wasn't actually meaning to be scary. He was lonely and was running after us because he just wanted some friends to play with.

My own spirituality and theology have been shaped over the last thirty years by, among others, Una Kroll and the late Michael Mayne. In conversation and correspondence they both helped me to learn to 'offer up' my experiences in solidarity with and on behalf of others in a kind of 'cosmic' intercessory way. To turn honestly and trustingly towards the living God in the face of your own pain can help, in some way, to intercede for countless unknown, unnamed, others who may be experiencing similar pain and anguish.

As I write, I am mindful of the many couples for whom hopes of conceiving and carrying to term a child are never realized; and those who never find the longed-for relationship that might lead to such a possibility; and those who lose a precious child at some later stage. Rob Bell articulated a truth that I have been groping towards through these last fifteen years when he explored the notion that, in the face of suffering, it is far more productive to ask, 'What now?', rather than expending too much energy on 'Why?' Suffering will shape us, he says; the question is, will we become 'bitter or better'?[109]

On 11 September 2001, when Clare was just fifteen months old, we were visiting my mother-in-law. We came home from a walk and found a message asking me to ring my mother. She sounded worried. All sorts of scenarios went through my head as I dialled her number. Her first words were, 'Rich's in that building.' I had no idea what she was talking about and she told me to turn on the television. I stared in disbelief as I saw the images of the aeroplanes flying into the buildings. My brother is married to an American woman. Her brother worked for Cantor Fitzgerald in the World Trade Centre. Like so many people, our lives were changed for ever that day. Rich's parents later asked if I would take part in the Memorial Service planned for the end of the month. There could not be a funeral because there was no body. He had been blown apart. (Years later small pieces of his DNA were identified among the remains.) I flew to the USA for four days with my mother,

109 Rob Bell, *Drops Like Stars*, Zondervan, 2009, pp. 118–19.

leaving Clare at home with her father. It was one of the hardest things I have ever done. Rich, his parents and my sister-in-law are all people of faith. Working in New York, Rich had also done voluntary work with the homeless through his church. He was an extraordinarily generous soul whose life had touched many people. There were some eight hundred people at the Memorial Service at his old school. I talked with young people there who were attending five or six or more such events over a week or two, as they mourned the friends and colleagues that they had lost.

I struggle to articulate an adequate theology in the face of the enormity of that day in 2001. The senseless blowing apart of lives cannot be explained away. I am also left thinking of the equally senseless scandal of the numbers of people dying day by day in our world because of a lack of clean water or basic medicines. Where is God in all this? I struggle with verses such as the following: 'For surely I know the plans I have for you, says the Lord, plans for your welfare and not for harm, to give you a future with hope' (Jeremiah 29.11).

After interring the cremated remains of an elderly lady one day in the late 1990s, I spoke to members of her extended family. One, Janet, with a babe in arms, spoke of how her child, Louisa, was named after the elderly aunt. It transpired that she had struggled with miscarriage before her daughter's birth. She worked as a theatre sister and some months later, by a quirk of fate, she was the one to accompany me back to the ward after one of my post-miscarriage operations. She sat with me for a while. Just a week after that, I had a phone call from Janet to say that she was now a patient on that same ward. It was my turn to sit beside her as she grieved the loss of twins. Our lives were entwined and later our daughters played together at the weekly Tots' Church. She went on to have a little boy as well. Only a couple of years later Janet became unwell. No one seemed to be able to get to diagnose what was wrong but Janet knew instinctively how serious things were. She sat in the Vicarage kitchen one day and asked directly: 'Jane, why has God given me these two beautiful children, after all my struggles, if he's now not going to let me live to see them grow up?'

We hugged and we wept together. A month or so later she was in a hospital bed unable to move or speak. She clung to me when I visited her. She died shortly afterwards, aged 45. I have watched her children grow up as they have been at the same school as Clare. I sometimes go and stand by Janet's grave to tell her how beautiful her children are and I weep.

I can (on a good day) draw strength from the verse that I regularly proclaim at the beginning of funeral services: 'The Lord gives and the Lord takes away. Blessed be the name of the Lord.' A doctor, working at the hospice where I was chaplain, told me one day about her experience of pregnancy loss and she drew my attention to the song 'Blessed be Your Name' (by Christian singer-songwriter Matt Redman), which she had found to be both a comfort and a challenge. Redman sings, 'My heart will choose to say, "Lord, blessed be your name".' The challenge is to go on choosing this not just when the sun is 'shining down' and when 'streams of abundance flow', but also when you find yourself 'in the desert place' or when 'the darkness closes in'. Job says: 'Naked I came from my mother's womb, and naked shall I return there; the Lord gave, and the Lord has taken away; blessed be the name of the Lord' (Job 1.21).

St Paul writes of boasting in sufferings, 'knowing that suffering produces endurance, and endurance produces character, and character produces hope, and hope does not disappoint us, because God's love has been poured into our hearts through the Holy Spirit that has been given to us' (Romans 5.3–5). There is a well-known children's story that can be read as a kind of commentary on these verses, *The Velveteen Rabbit (Or How Toys Become Real)*. I was first given a copy by a nun friend in the early 1980s. Being open to being loved and to loving makes us vulnerable or, in the case of the Velveteen Rabbit or his companion, the old Skin Horse, battered and somewhat shabby:

> Generally, by the time you are Real, most of your hair has been loved off, and your eyes drop out and you get loose in the joints and very shabby. But these things don't matter at

> all, because once you are Real you can't be ugly, except to people who don't understand.[110]

We live in a culture which is focused on success and perfection and which is also very uncomfortable about the realities of death. Newspaper articles speak of a 'cure for cancer' as if it will somehow make us immortal. The Christian faith is very clear that death is not the end of our soul's journey. And our suffering saviour challenges our notions of success and power.

I have always felt deep discomfort at the notion that 'this is all part of God's plan for you'. I believe that redemption is always possible. I have come to believe that with God 'no life or love – even the smallest seed – is ever wasted'.[111] I cannot now remember the first time I came across the metaphor of life as a tapestry, composed of threads of different colours and lengths. It was suggested that I consider all the loose and untidy threads which are to be found at the back of a beautiful, delicately shaded, tapestry. Without them the picture could not be composed.[112]

One of the strange, redemptive twists that my journey has taken is that I now do occasional input to midwifery training. I met the Head of Midwifery from our local University Hospital at a party and was reflecting with her on the impact of some of the good and bad experiences of midwifery that I had encountered, both through

---

110 Margery Williams, with illustrations by William Nicholson, *The Velveteen Rabbit (Or How Toys Become Real)*, Corgi Carousel, 1976, reprint 1978, p. 9. The book was first published in Great Britain by Heinemann in 1922.

111 Rees (ed.), *Voices of this Calling*, p.113.

112 A number of people attribute this to Corrie Ten Boom in a 'Tapestry Poem', which begins, 'My life is but a weaving between my God and me', and includes the words:

> Oft' times He weaveth sorrow;
> and I in foolish pride
> forget He sees the upper
> and I the underside.

'Tapestrychurch', attributed to Corrie Ten Boom, www.tapestrychurch.net/blog_tapestry.

my multiple miscarriages and through being a 'birth partner'. She asked if I would be prepared to lead a session from a 'user' perspective for trainee midwives in their final term. I have done that a couple of times now and it has proved to be a rich and emotional encounter. One group invited me back to their final session before graduation and asked me to bless their hands for the work that they were going out to do.

Witnessing my grief and sense of loss parishioners would ask, 'What have you ever done to deserve this?' They saw me as a fundamentally 'good' person and so they struggled with a sense that my suffering was somehow being directly caused by God and must therefore be some kind of punishment. As I saw the same thought processes at work in many of the carers I came into contact with through my work in the hospice I began to use the term 'Father-Christmas theology' as a kind of shorthand for this way of seeing things. The God I love and trust (and who I believe loves and trusts me) does not operate like that. Our God does not withhold gifts in order to punish us. In Jesus, God walks with us, weeps with us, and leads us to dance with thanksgiving and forgiveness 'at all times and in all places'. As I preside at eucharistic worship, again and again I am led to give thanks for all that I am being given and I am challenged to forgive life, to forgive God, to forgive others for not giving me all that I might desire.

Our daughter is now twelve years old. We delight in her sheer existence. She went away on a residential music weekend just recently with our local County Music Service. We went to the concert on the Sunday lunchtime and watched her playing her flute alongside forty or so other young people on a whole range of instruments. As they struck up the first piece and the sound filled the great entrance hall of the old stately home turned arts centre where they had been staying, I wept. I felt so moved by what I could see and hear. And in the midst of it there was Clare, already looking so confident and accomplished. Pure gift. And I found myself asking, 'What have I ever done to deserve this?'

5

A Burden not to be Borne[113]

CHRISTOPHER FINLAY

So often it is the insignificant events in life that ultimately produce the most profound effects. Trivial things can increase imperceptibly until they become a major influence on everything else, reaching to the foundations of life and faith. All our accepted priorities are thrown into disarray and the security of faith which we have attained is thrown wide open. We are faced with a radical reappraisal of our relationship with God and the way in which his power works in our lives.

For me this all began with a toothache; not the violent, throbbing type usually associated with tooth troubles, but rather a dull, persistent irritation above one tooth. After several, expensive treatments from the dentist there was no improvement and the problem was starting to enflame nerves behind my ear and eye. I asked to see the dental consultant at the local hospital.

The maxillo-facial surgeon was brisk but kind. He quickly ascertained there was nothing wrong with the dentistry so sent me for an X-ray of my whole head. At the appointment a week later the film on the display showed an ominous black mark in the jaw above my teeth and it was clear there was some sort of problem. The surgeon made a list of five headings and then said that it would be necessary to do a biopsy under general anaesthetic, to establish exactly what was going on. He would not be drawn into discussing the possible diagnosis but the operation would be scheduled for two weeks' time. It began to dawn upon me that this might be serious. The speed with which things were to go forward, the quiet kindness of the

113 W. B. Yeats, 'Under the Moon'.

surgeon and that ominous X-ray all pointed to something I would rather not think about.

All this came at a time when great changes were taking place in my life and the future had begun to open up in way I had not considered possible a year or two before. I had been ordained for three years, had taken early retirement and was settling into a non-stipendiary parish ministry which was proving most satisfying, plus serving on the Diocesan Finance Committee. It was a full and exciting period with new opportunities. I had first sought ordination many years before but God had seemed to say 'not yet'. I had contented myself with a rewarding Reader ministry and assumed that was where I would remain. A friend prompted me to try again and to my great surprise God opened the possibility I had come to consider closed. It seemed inconceivable that things would go wrong in such an unexpected way, after all, his calling seemed clear, why should it be blocked?

As I sat waiting for the biopsy I was no more anxious than one normally is for a minor procedure. A friend had lent me a book on the 'Jesus Prayer', written by a Russian monk,[114] as an explanation of how that prayer could be used to aid contemplation; it proved useful to help me commit myself to God's care. Looking back, I realize there was an element of denial involved that day. I knew very well that biopsies were associated with cancer diagnoses but preferred not to acknowledge it.

Shortly afterwards I found myself before the surgeon in the same state of confidence; it was not to last. He was kind but direct; the news was not good, I had an adenoid cystic carcinoma in my sinus and it was malignant. He was sorry, it was the last thing he had put on that list and he had hoped it would not be relevant. I don't recall being very shocked or afraid, simply that I seemed to have entered a void over which I had no control. I suppose subconsciously I knew that the black mark on the X-ray had meant it was very serious; now the element

114 Anon, E. M. French (trans.), *The Way of a Pilgrim*, reprint, HarperCollins, 1997.

of denial had been removed. The surgeon went on to say that it was rare type of cancer for which the only treatment was 'radical surgery and extreme radiotherapy'. There was a pause to gauge my reaction and I was offered some tea. When they were sure that I had not lost my composure, the surgeon went on to say that the next step would be an MRI scan, to establish the extent of the tumour, he would then be able to plan the operation. He fetched a teaching aid skull and explained that the procedure involved opening up my cheek so that half my upper jaw could be removed to gain access to the cancer in the sinus. Afterwards I would have to wear an extended dental plate to compensate for the loss of the jaw and hard palate. The operation would be followed by a course of radiotherapy. He explained that the procedure was standard, although they did not do it very often, but it would be traumatic. I need not have the operation if I did not want to but he felt, that at fifty-three, I had no real option. His prognosis was eighteen months without surgery and probably ten years if the work was done. That was about all the information I could absorb. I was sent to have an immediate chest X-ray to ensure there was no secondary cancer in my lungs and would receive the MRI scan appointment as a matter of urgency.

I emerged a little dazed, and had to wait until after lunch for the X-ray. Patty had not come with me to the appointment as neither of us had expected such a diagnosis. I did not want to tell her by phone but had no option, because she was expecting me home and would worry when I did not appear. It was a very difficult call, as were the calls to the children to tell them. For all of us the shock was quite numbing and we sought reassurance, both practical and spiritual, in trying to understand how things would go forward.

Prayer was the immediate response, more for understanding of what was going on than anything else; the position of Job suddenly became very real indeed. Why had this happened? Was there some sort of point to it? Where was God in it all? What did the future hold, apart from what the doctors described? These are all the usual questions that arise when disaster strikes and reactions vary from anger and resentment at God for 'allowing' it to happen, with the anger preceding a renunciation of faith, to a stoical acceptance or fatalistic denial of reality. Strangely, I found no anger, no real fear even. There is no cessation of Our Lord's presence (Matthew 28.20) unless we choose to remove ourselves because of confusion or anger, and it was this assurance which provided a stable ground for dealing with catastrophe.

The MRI scan took place a few days later and a week afterwards we were back to hear what would happen. The basic facts about the treatment were repeated but now that we were prepared, more details were added. The scan showed the tumour was quite large, having been there for some years. The surgeon felt he could remove it all but warned that if it went too far into the fragile structures behind the eye and nose the risks of fatal haemorrhage would be too high. Access would be through the front of my face but I was assured scarring would become invisible after a short period of time. I would be unable to eat, so would be fed by tube while in hospital and would need to see the dietician. The extended dental type plate, to fill the gap and seal the opening created in the sinus would be done in a stop-gap measure during the operation, to be replaced by a more precise fitment when the surgery trauma had subsided. The bad news was that I would probably be unable to speak properly and would need speech therapy. About three months after the operation, the long course of radiotherapy would begin. The oncologist explained that this type of cancer spread through the nerves and even when removed it was essential to follow up in this way, to try and ensure that no trace was left behind to be transferred as a secondary cancer. There was no evidence this had happened yet, so the prospects seemed good.

The operation was arranged for about a month later. It would be long and complicated with intensive care after, so once fixed, the date could not be changed. We would just have time for the holiday in Cornwall we had already arranged. The speed of events stunned us. We realized that not only was this very serious but life in the future was going to be governed by circumstances beyond our control, with no certainty about how things would turn out. There were echoes of Jesus' prophecy to Peter about being taken where he did not wish to go (John 21.18).

We went home bemused and set about telling the family and our friends. Their response was shock, followed by much care and sympathy. We were touched by the depth of concern and the amount of prayer support from the parishes and my colleague Canon Tony Ross; it was encouraging to know they would be there for us as events unfolded. The more evangelical group among us urged me to come to a special prayer meeting to invoke healing. This was not something I was entirely comfortable with. I have always been ambivalent about this approach to healing ministry. I have seen events of people wonderfully restored by prayer and of others greatly helped, though not cured, but remain unconvinced that this intense approach to healing is the right route. It may conform to the exhortation in James (James 5.14–15) and to Jesus' declaration to his disciples (John 14.14) that whatever they ask in his name will be given, but it ignores the pressure such an approach puts upon the sufferer. There is a very real danger of raising expectations of a quick miracle cure, with the reverse consequence of despair when this does not occur. Too often the person prayed for is left with the feeling that their faith is not good enough or that God has abandoned them. We need to approach healing in a more humble way, laying our distress before God in the knowledge that he will walk with us in suffering. There is a place for structured prayer for healing within our church communities, but it ought to be as a continuous practice, invoking trust and love rather than commanding God to perform miracles.

There were practical things to do as well – more hospital tests and arrangments for my nine-month absence from duty. I did not have time to reflect much on the larger implications because the immediate future and how to deal with that was the main feature. For me, that provided a focus, whereas for the rest of the family there was not only the surgery to contemplate but also the longer-term implications, the possibility of things not working out as hoped, and the waiting. It is always harder for those loved ones who must sit and watch and wait. There was only a limited amount of support I could give in return, because they, understandably, felt they could not talk to me about all their concerns. Our week in Cornwall doing familiar things in familiar places allowed us some relief from all this intensity, we returned as ready as we could be for what had to be.

Sitting in my hospital room waiting to walk across the corridor to the operating theatre, knowing I would not return to consciousness for two days and that nothing afterwards would be quite the same, was a bizarre experience. There was mild anxiety but no real fear. Prayer was barely possible, but I had by now accepted that I could only place everything in the Lord's hands and trust him to sustain me through it, and at no time did I feel alone.

I came round with an intense pain in my face and registering that the clock on the wall said ten minutes to four. An unseen IC nurse was reassuring me I was fine and giving me a pain control handset, telling me how to depress it to release more morphine as I needed it. I replied to her and was amazed to realize I could speak clearly enough for her to understand all I said without difficulty. This was the first of many blessings I was to find in the weeks and years to come. The next few days were a bit of a blur, the result of the medication, but slowly things cleared. The fourth day was the worst, the usual down day after surgery when you wish it had never been done; it was aggravated by my being unable to tolerate the feeding tube any longer. A heated discussion ensued about how I would manage while unable to eat when I refused to have it put back. With the help and endless kindness of the staff, plus that of family and visiting friends, we managed. After eleven days I went home to begin the long, slow process of recovery.

These were not days of intense prayer or reflection. Such are not possible when one is so debilitated; it was much more a time to 'wait without thought, for you are not ready for thought'.[115] It was sufficient to know there was a great deal of prayer being offered and to be thankful for the enduring presence of Christ. Another source of strength was the Psalms, with their expressions of deep personal experience of all conditions of life and understanding of God's ways. Here in the hope and rejoicing, suffering and despair, trust in God's holiness and striving to understand events, I found a place to rest and hope. The sense of oneness with the writer brought new understanding to Psalms I had merely been accustomed to in the past. Psalm 23 became a reality; 71 a place of comfort; 130 for understanding; 63 for thanksgiving, and many more. This was living scripture in which to find a future again.

Over the next three months I regained a measure of physical strength and began to come to terms with the malfunctions of my mouth which made it difficult to eat, drink and speak. There was a series of minor procedures to stabilize things, which alleviated many of the problems, although eating and drinking would always be difficult. The care from friends and family and the endless gifts of ice cream were mainstays of recovery, giving a positive prospect to the future. It was with pleasure that I was able to have some parish and social life.

This was only the halfway house though; there was still the radiotherapy to come. The doctors had made clear the need for this. As the nerves in my eye and ear had been inflamed, it was imperative to try to destroy any cells the surgery had not removed. I did not want to go back into the world of illness and was less than positive about more treatment. They were tolerant and encouraging, while adamant this was as essential as the surgery; I knew I had to trust to their skill, despite my anxiety. The procedure would last four weeks, with sessions five days a week. The side effects would be harsh. The main problems would be burning of the skin, like severe sunburn, and burning inside my throat, which would make eating difficult. The preparations were most trying, involving making a face mask

115 T. S. Eliot 'East Coker', *Complete Poems and Plays*, Faber, 2004.

on which to mark the target areas, followed by an hour of total immobility, while the calculations were made. For the first time the questions about why this had occurred began to arise. As always, there could be no complete answer in the rational terms we would like.

The treatment itself was painless but the side effects were cumulative. After the first two weeks these began to build up and gradually I was moved on to stronger pain killers. I managed, just, with the last weeks of treatment, the two or three weeks afterwards passing in a vague drug-induced haze. In many ways it was worse than the surgery. I was relieved when it was done, although a stone lighter in weight. The extreme treatment was over, it was now time to recover strength and come to terms with the artificial mouth plate, which would make it possible to live reasonably normally again. This was a great trial to begin with but as the tissue damage healed it became possible to make something that fitted more comfortably. Generally, we do not have to think of the part our mouth plays in living. To find it difficult to do the normal things like eating, drinking and speaking in a spontaneous way is quite a restriction upon daily living. It would never be a perfect solution and I have learned to live with the discomfort over the years. But at least there was a future.

All this intense activity had taken place over eight months, when past and future had been suspended and the present had been wholly consumed by survival. Spiritually, I had found a changed understanding of the way in which God meets us in our lives. In the closeness of Christ, in even the darkest times, that distance between us and God, which we strive so hard to cross through prayer and in other ways, had been removed. There still remained the inevitable questions which we find we have to confront; why do we have to deal with suffering? Where is God in suffering? What does it all mean in terms of ministry and the future? It had not been appropriate to deal with these before but now was the time.

'Why suffering?' is one of the questions all clergy are faced with most frequently. People are quick to say that their faith has been ruined by suffering – sometimes their own, more often that of a loved one. The cry is always, 'How can a loving God allow this?', or, 'Why does he not instantly put it right in response to prayer, as promised?' Both are as much cries of desolation as reasonable questions; they look for immediate solutions to the immediate problem, but in our terms. In scripture this is dealt with in Job in the context of the ancient belief that suffering was the inevitable consequence of religious failure. It does indeed show God tolerating Job's suffering, but as a construct for developing the overall problem of how we deal with suffering. I do not believe that God ever deliberately causes suffering for humanity; neither is suffering a form of judgement. We do bring suffering on ourselves or inflict it on others by our own actions, but in the main I have come to accept that most suffering is part of the essence of being. We are created beings that must die, there is no avoiding this, neither is there a guarantee of how long we are given, nor are we assured that our passage will always be comfortable. We tell people death is part of life not the end, and conversely we must accept that in life we must deal with suffering. The real question is how do we learn to deal with suffering in the context of our faith and of God's loving promises?

In Job the discussion swings backwards and forwards, attempting to define why Job is so afflicted. Job refuses to condemn God but ultimately feels he can reasonably ask for an explanation from God. In his response, God seems to give no answer to Job's request. But how can we demand account from God when we are his creation? To do so separates us from God in a way that destroys the basis of trust God seeks to create between himself and us. Instead of an answer, God demonstrates (by comparison of relationships) that to have faith is the fulfilment of life and therefore absolute trust is the only basis of a complete life. Answers lie in the relationship, not in a justification required of one party.

The essence of being is independence through dependence: freedom through gift of God: identity through acknowledgement of God as our creator. Therefore we are who we are and can be what we might be only in union with God. For God to be God is sufficient. Trust is the ultimate ground for knowing him. Without doubt, that trust is tested most severely in suffering but when we abandon ourselves to the promised love, we come to a deeper understanding of ourselves and how much God seeks to engage with our lives.

This still leaves us with trying to understand how to deal with the realities of suffering, how to find that deeper level of trust at times of distress and how do we hold on to it when circumstances improve? We all find different ways of probing these difficult depths and for me the road of St John of the Cross was the most revealing. I had struggled for years to find a satisfactory practice of contemplation, not as a personal attribute but as a foundation for a better life of faith. I generally came to grief on my inability to clear my mind sufficiently to progress. Nevertheless, the principle of being drawn into holiness by exclusion of self had remained an attractive means of knowing God better.

John is concerned chiefly with attaining a greater awareness of God's presence through contemplation. In *Dark Night of the Soul*[116] he describes a progression of thought which gradually replaces self-concern with an emptying of the soul, so that we can begin to understand the true nature of God. John's central tenet is the need to strip away all dependence on earthly things. Complete abandonment to the love of God is imperative; without it, our participation in holiness can never be complete. The difficulty is how to attain this state within the drama of ordinary life. For John, contemplation is the route, for others disaster can have a similar effect. When events remove all the props and silence all the semantics which clutter our relationship with God, we find ourselves face to face with an unavoidable reconsideration of the way we understand faith. 'Can I really abandon all to his loving care?' No matter how much we acknowledge God's power and glory, it is a significant step to accept him fully for what he is and allow ourselves to be

116 St John of the Cross, *Dark Night of the Soul*, Dover, 2003.

led by him – a step we are often unwilling to take of our own volition. That is not to say that to take that step removes all the complications which beset living faithfully. It is much more a revelation from which we understand more deeply God's love, allowing us to go on in a more peaceful and purposeful way. I do not claim any special revelation with this, or the achievement of some pinnacle of spiritual grace such as the medieval mystics sought, rather it is about finding a level of acceptance and hope through Christ, which makes the present manageable and the future possible. In scriptural terms nothing 'will be able to separate us from the love of God' (Romans 8.39).

This was the level I found to deal with my illness. It did not, however, offer much help to my family as they cared for me, other than that if I was reasonably positive they would find their own pain easier to deal with. There is an inevitable gap between patient and carers, born of the struggle to deal with one's own suffering and mortality. The watchers feel all the anxiety of being unable to influence the situation very much and they have to live with the uncertainty of the future. Their loving care had been instrumental in my being able to get through; now, as recovery got under way, we could face the future together. We were under no illusion that recovery could mean a return to old normality. We had no guarantee that the treatment would completely defeat the cancer, and we realized that I would never be quite as able to do all that I had done before. It was a case of living each day as it came; trying to ignore any anxieties about what might go wrong and giving thanks for the small miracles of progress that occurred, such as the recovery of good speech and the ability to live a normal life again.

This was also the time to resume ministry. Ministry did not present itself in quite the way it had been because parishioners and friends had been supporting me with their prayer and help for many months; our relationship had changed. I decided that I would be completely open about the cancer and its treatment, in the hope that such frankness would enable others to feel more able to use me to deal with their own afflictions.

This proved to be what happened. There have been numerous occasions when it has been possible to talk through and offer prayer with others as they face the reality of cancer. It was as if sharing that state with others gave them permission to confront their own fears in the context of God, rather than alone. I find I have been able to give them courage and confidence. They also challenged me on some of the big questions. Was my faith damaged, if not why not? Why had God let this happen? Could a miracle be expected? No, my faith was not damaged, it had been strengthened because there is no other source of hope. The others are eternal questions, to which I am convinced there are no standard answers in the form the questioner expects. In so far as trying to reason why God seems to permit suffering, it is the assumption on which the question is based which is wrong. The right question is 'where is God in all this?' Many do have a fixation with being cured instantly, as the Gospel accounts describe, in answer to prayer. Looking back after the event, there are many little miracles in what occurred, but not in this one expected manner. More often they are lights into a better understanding of God and of our neighbours that enrich our lives, and it becomes part of ministry to explain this.

The six years that followed were relatively stable health-wise, allowing me to develop my ministry and take on the Chair of the Board of Finance for the Diocese. The doctors were quietly confident that we had passed the five-year threshold, but kept up regular reviews. It was at one of these that I had to tell them that there seemed to be an abnormality in my neck. Scans revealed a small tumour, which tests confirmed was the same type as before. A major operation on my neck was carried out to remove it, but this went well and did not present the same recovery problems as before. The very bad news was that there were also small lung tumours, which were untreatable but very slow growing; they would not pose a problem for several years. We were shocked that the cancer had returned, this time with no prospect of cure. Again, it was the family who were hit hardest by the news. I had subconsciously acknowledged that the warnings given six years before were being borne out. The best thing to do was to get on with life as it was, trusting in God's mercy. We had an interregnum at that time and I resolved to resign the Diocesan role as soon as my new parochial colleague arrived and the synod triennium expired, so that I could spend more time with the family. There was still no anger with God, however, the relentlessness of the disease, its low-level pain and the seeming irrelevance of the future can evoke an element of depression. I felt a bit like Jeremiah at this stage, asking why things had to be this way and what was it that was expected of me. Always I received the same reply, 'my grace is sufficient for you' (2 Corinthians 12.9).

There was not a great deal of respite because, within eighteen months, the neck tumour reappeared and was much larger. The scans showed it to be deeply embedded and the surgeon had to tell me it was inoperable because the mortality risk was too high. There was only prayer left now, and again it was answered. The oncologist calculated that it was just possible to apply more radiotherapy to shrink the tumour without endangering the area close by that had already been irradiated. It was another extreme course of thirty-four sessions. I felt some trepidation at the thought of a repeat but, mercifully, it was lower down my neck, so the side effects were less acute, although not trivial. The tumour has shrunk, which has bought some more time, as the rate of growth is expected to be slow. Life has changed perceptibly. I am living with a fact rather than a probability, something finite rather than remote. Surprisingly, it does not make a great deal of difference from a faith and trust point of view. In the context of Christ's ever-present love the question 'Why?' remains irrelevant. Theologically I find myself less moved by the pure theological concept of justification by faith in the merits of Christ and more at home in a deeper immersion in Christ through grace alone. That grace remains present and sufficient. There is still much to do and much to rejoice in and I give thanks for this in the manner of John Keble, 'New ev'ry morning'.[117] It does mean that the more trivial trials of

117 *Hymns Old & New*, Kevin Mayhew, 2004.

life can be dismissed when, in the past, they occupied much attention; I must also beware of becoming slightly detached from ordinary things around me, which can separate me from those who love me. It has taken a long time to reach the point which Eliot describes as 'a condition of complete simplicity costing not less than everything'[118] and in that light I will accept things as they happen.

118 T. S. Eliot, 'Little Gidding', *Complete Poems and Plays*.

6

The Passing of Time

JOHN CLARKE

It was on the ferry back from the Isle of Wight that I acknowledged, finally, that I was seriously ill and needed to see a doctor. The car deck on the ferry was connected to the sitting area by two steep flights of stairs and I nearly didn't make it up them. On the car journey back to Wells I felt ghastly, and first thing the next morning Cressida phoned the doctor. Dr Goddard came to visit me at home and asked me to tell the story of what had happened. He listened to my chest. 'Do you know you have a heart murmur?' he asked. He telephoned the local hospitals and managed that evening to get me admitted to Musgrove Park in Taunton.

I say admitted, but in fact I spent four hours sitting and lying on the floor in the reception area for new patients before a bed was found. Then, a few hours later, on 31 March 2008, I was transferred to a cardiac ward, where I stayed for three weeks.

Looking back, I could see that the first sign of illness was in November 2006 when I couldn't shake off what I took to be a persistent virus. I think of myself as an active person. I enjoy mountain walking, cycling, playing cricket. Throughout 2007 my energy levels were low and I tired quickly. We went on holiday to Holland, a house exchange with a Dutch family, and when we borrowed their bikes to go cycling, even on mainly flat roads, I found it hard work. But at that point I didn't want to acknowledge that there was anything wrong. My mind and will tried to blot out any hint that my body might need help.

But in March 2008 my body went on strike. I took time off work thinking that this was exhaustion and that I would soon recover, especially with the prospect of our usual, post-Easter week's holiday on the Isle of Wight. But then I started to get panic attacks which I had never experienced in my life before. They were deeply frightening. I would go from my bedroom to the bathroom but as I went to urinate I found it impossible to breathe and the room would start to spin. I feared that I would collapse. My fear was that I would die during one of the attacks. Cressida, who is a musician, encouraged me to sing, because if you sing you have to breathe. My repertoire of hymns worked to some extent and I was, at least for a few moments, able to trick my mind to let me make the short journey back to my bed in safety. As chaos threatened to overwhelm, hymns reassured me of an ordered and familiar world, a world held by God. Singing had its comic side; as I would belt out the first verse of 'Praise my soul the king of heaven' or 'All my hope on God is founded' the children knew that this was just Dad on the loo.

But to go back to November 2006 is not really to go back far enough, because I am sure that physical, psychological and spiritual accounts of this illness are necessary in order to begin to see the picture of what was happening.

I had moved to Wells in July 2004 and started as Dean in September. My previous job had been as Principal of Ripon College Cuddesdon, training men and women for ordained ministry, mainly in the Church of England. The move to Wells had been difficult. I wondered if it was the right time for me to leave the college with important changes afoot that led to the college incorporating the Oxford Ministry Course and the Oxford Local Ministry Scheme. I had no previous experience of ministry in an English cathedral and wasn't sure how I would manage within the formality of cathedral worship. Eventually I was convinced by the fact that the 'note', that served as a job description, from William Chapman, the Prime Minister's Appointments Secretary, indicated the need for the new Dean to have skills that seemed a good match for mine. Even so, I delayed moving because the College was celebrating 150 years of its existence.

More importantly, my family was divided about the move. My older son Ben, then aged fifteen, was eager to come to Wells and go to the Cathedral School. Edmund (twelve) and Esther (ten) were upset at the thought of leaving Cuddesdon and their current schools. Cressida had struggled with bouts of severe depression for many years and came to feel that the thought of moving and setting up home again in another large house was impossible. After much discussion, Ben and I moved to Wells in the Summer of 2004. Cressida, Edmund and Esther stayed in the little house in Wheatley we had bought from the College, commuting to Wells most weekends and during the school holidays. It was a painful time in family life, resolved during the following year when Esther became a chorister at the cathedral, and Cressida's depression worsened towards incapacitation. In January 2006 Cressida and Edmund decided that the only course of action was to take the plunge and start afresh in Wells.

My work as Dean was demanding. Richard Lewis, my predecessor, and John Roberts, the Cathedral administrator, had driven forward a comprehensive and imaginative development scheme; the new works would enable the Cathedral to be run more effectively and make it more accessible to the 300,000 visitors who come to Wells each year. Planning permission had been achieved before Richard retired and a substantial sum of money had been raised. But the actual building work had not yet started. The new Dean, together with the administrator, was expected to see the project to completion.

During 2005, builders were engaged who, thankfully, worked well with the architects and the Cathedral Clerk of Works. A part-time fundraiser was employed to raise the remaining £3 million that was needed. But, inevitably, with a project of this complexity in a busy working cathedral, there were complications to be addressed: costs needed to be held down and specifications reduced; colleagues on the Chapter and different departments of the Cathedral had to be consulted; letters of application had to be written, forms filled in and visits arranged for the Heritage Lottery Fund and other grant-making trusts.

All this was on top of the day-to-day work of a Dean, a role which requires liturgical and preaching skills, a sense of strategic leadership, and the ability to cooperate and adjudicate between a wide range of groups who have a stake in the life of a cathedral. In the midst of the whirl of activity the Dean has to be a still centre, part of the Chapter whose ordained members meet daily for morning and evening prayer, and who together embody the inner purpose of the Cathedral as a witness to the love of God for people of all faiths and none, the love that Christians believe is focused in the life, death, and resurrection of Jesus.

Another major part of the Dean's role at Wells is chairing the governing body of the Cathedral School, a surprisingly time-consuming and complex job. The school is in the independent sector and has 700 pupils, a mixture of day pupils and boarders, ranging from three to eighteen years. It educates the choristers of the Cathedral, both boys and girls, and has a specialist music focus as one of the five schools in Britain where the Government subsidizes places for musicians with exceptional talent. This makes for an exciting musical environment and a creative school community. Giving time to it as a governor is very worthwhile.

The first years of my time at Wells had been a time of conflict within the governing body. The tension erupted at a meeting where one governor made a prepared speech against the head, resigned, and left. The remaining governors were shocked at the manner of his departure. As chair of the governors I both needed to support the head and to listen to the issues of concern which were shared by some other governors. It was an uncomfortable place to sit, and, although the governing body is now united behind the head, the pressure of the conflict took its toll. I had to chair a tense series of meetings to agree a way forward. I tend to take conflict into myself and feel that I should be able to resolve it. When I can't, I wake in the middle of the night worrying and find it difficult to get back to sleep.

The relationship between Cathedral and Diocese is never easy to get right. Ideally there should be a supportive and creative dialogue between both parties. Maintaining clear boundaries between the tasks of the Bishop and the tasks of the Chapter is a constant challenge. The Dean is always the spokesperson for the Chapter. Issues of personality and structure can become deeply interwoven. Here, too, I found that, at certain times, I could not cut off from issues that had surfaced, and would turn them over again and again in my mind during the night.

Behind these family and work pressures lay the critical question of how I handled stress and anger. Even if I could absorb the anger of others quite instinctively, I found it much more difficult to admit to and deal with my own anger, especially when I felt exposed or accused by others. In particular, how did I deal with the anger of other people when that anger was directed towards me? Anger is closely connected with stress, and stress with heart conditions. How could I combine the multiple roles I played as husband, father, dean, chair of governors, chair of the trustees of the City of Wells Almshouses, member of Bishop's Staff, and a spiritual director, without constant overwork? How, in my soul, when I was tired and doubtful of my own judgement could I believe that I was loved, and loveable? My first reaction under pressure is to feel that I need to prove myself by my works, my actions, decisions and words, to show that I am more capable than others. Such a response does not give much room for the grace of God to work.

All of these different tensions came together and led me to a hospital bed in Taunton. While I was there, I was diagnosed with two conditions – a badly leaking mitral heart valve, which explained my complete loss of energy, and atrial fibrillation which accounted for the panic attacks. Atrial fibrillation meant that my pulse would race before returning to a more normal level. Both of them would require surgery, though the atrial fibrillation could be alleviated by the use of drugs. Surgery meant referral to a consultant in Bristol and an unknown period of waiting.

My stay at Musgrove Park was my first extended time in hospital. I had to face fears about what was wrong with my heart, and what, if anything could be done about it. More immediately, I had to face my fear of injections! I realized how quickly I became dependent on the routines of hospital life – pills, meals, consultants' rounds and visits. In the cardiac wards at Musgrove Park the staff was overstretched, and nursing relied heavily on agency staff. I met real kindness from staff, but also saw moments when human dignity was ignored or forgotten, including one instance of cruelty when a frail eighty-year-old man was kept sitting in a chair for three hours because staff were too busy to change the mattress of his bed to the type that he had been promised. It was a salutary change to move from my role as Dean to be a person without status and with little power. For the nurses I was probably a pleasant but rather frightened man in the bed near the window; to the doctors who knew what I did at work I was a bit of a curiosity.

In this scaring and unfamiliar environment I couldn't sleep well. I tried to keep a wider sense of self by saying, morning and evening, a psalm and readings from the daily office, and when my mind was not too driven by anxiety, keeping a period of silence. I also tried to read, and especially remember reading the diaries of the young Dutch Jewish woman Etty Hillesum which were written during the Nazi occupation of Amsterdam, and then talking about them with Patrick, a colleague, who was writing a book about her.[119] The adversity she had faced, and the courage she showed, helped to keep my self-centred fears in perspective.

Back home my life had to take on a new routine. I decided to do some theological writing that had been in my mind for some time. I took over our upstairs living room in the morning, worked and listened to the radio. In the afternoon, when it was fine, I would venture out into the garden. If Cressida and the children were around they would stop by from time to time to see how I was getting on. I was not up to cooking, and was

---

119 Klaas A. D. Smith (ed.), Arnold J. Pomerans (trans.), *Etty: The Letters and Diaries of Etty Hillesum 1941–43*, Eerdmans, 2002; Patrick Woodhouse, *Etty Hillesum: A Life Transformed*, Continuum, 2009.

aware that all the responsibility for feeding the family fell on Cressida, on top of her work as musician and teacher.

I received lots of cards and messages of support and knew that many people in the Cathedral, and further afield, were praying for me. I had sent out a message to the Cathedral congregation saying no visits, for fear that their genuine concern for me would overwhelm, and that I also would fall back into the role of pastor and carer. When I felt able I would go and sit at the back of the Sunday Eucharist, but sometimes when I did, I found that being in the Cathedral brought on a renewed sense of panic. Perhaps the very power of the place, and the power of the Eucharist brought up fears that most of the time I would repress. Even the sense of people's care made me aware of expectations I could not meet. I might never be able to resume the role of Dean.

I was pleased to see my colleagues on the Chapter, and arranged that the Cathedral Administrator would come once a fortnight to keep me briefed on the Development Project and other Cathedral matters. I chose two people, Sr Carol CHN, who lived in Vicars Close beside the Cathedral, and Nicola Sullivan, Archdeacon of Wells and a member of the Chapter, to provide spiritual care. Sister Carol would come and pray with me usually once a week and Nicola would regularly celebrate Communion in my house. They upheld me and helped me to express my hopes and fears in this period where I swung between anxiety for myself and for my family – I am not ready to die, I have too much I want to do, was a constant inner refrain – and denial that this was more than a temporary reverse and my life would soon continue virtually uninterrupted. During this time I also worked with a counsellor to look at some of the work issues that provoked stress in me.

May was about waiting. June brought an angiogram back in Taunton, and then the consultant told me that he would refer me to a surgeon, Mr Ascione, in Bristol, who was a specialist in the repair of heart valves. Weeks passed and I heard nothing. It took repeated phone calls to the Taunton hospital to get the consultant to ring back. Eventually I discovered that the papers had not been sent. At this point, I sought the phone number of Mr Ascione and decided to call his secretary. She knew nothing of me. After further phone calls it was arranged for me to see Mr Ascione in July. He was a genial Italian doctor and was prepared to give plenty of time to discuss my case. He declared that he was nearly certain that the valve could be repaired rather than replaced. When I asked him what he would do he said, 'I might do one of twenty different things, it depends what I find when you are opened up!' I found it reassuring that he sounded more like an artist than a car mechanic. It felt that here were hands to whom I could entrust myself in this step into the unknown. A few days later the operation was fixed for 18 August. Cressida's parents came to be with the children. Cressida arranged to stay the night after the operation with friends in Bristol.

I was to report to the hospital at 8am on the day of the operation. It was also the day when Edmund, our second son, was due to receive his GCSE results. I wanted to hear how he had got on before being made unconscious. Fortunately, I was down the surgeon's list and the operation didn't take place until the middle of the day, and so was able to speak to Edmund and congratulate him. Gradually I was prepared for the operation and the anaesthetic. Shaving my chest ready for the incision was both comic and a significant step on the way. It all felt both frightening and slightly unreal as I had little idea of what lay ahead. Saying goodbye to Cressida, as I was wheeled out of the ward, was awful and I cried. Then, in a small room that seemed to be full of people, I was made to go unconscious. When I woke up, or perhaps it is more accurate to say, regained consciousness, I was in intensive care attached to drips and measuring devices.

The hours of the operation were the hardest time for Cressida and the children. Not knowing how to cope with the time Cressida decided to sit in a chapel of Bristol Cathedral, the oldest part of the building and a place set aside for silence and contemplative prayer. During the operation she moved between the chapel and the beautiful Cathedral garden where she could sit in the sunshine and have a cup of tea and a sandwich from the Cathedral café. It seemed fitting that another cathedral could offer a space of welcome at a time when she needed silence and holding.

One of the strangest parts of the experience of the operation for me was the sense that time had gone missing. There were perhaps five to six hours while I was unconscious which did not seem to fit into any sequence of time. It was a stretch of time when I was totally in the hands of other people, and when I had no control over what happened. It was not a sleep that I had chosen or that had come upon me because of tiredness. In that missing time something was done to perhaps the most intimate part of my body that has enabled me to recover and, at least until now, to live a full and busy life again.

For it seemed that the operation had been a success. The valve had been repaired with help from a cow and now leaked only a little. The atrial fibrillation had been tamed by what is called a 'Maze' procedure. Over the next few days when I returned to the cardiac ward, Cressida and the children came on daily visits. They were as relieved as I was. Gradually the wires were removed and the medication was reduced, though the pain where the cut had been made was considerable if I coughed or sneezed. Despite the signs that the doctors felt I was improving, I remained deeply anxious and would wake up several times during the night even though I was taking plenty of painkillers.

I didn't see Mr Ascione again until an appointment six weeks after I had gone home, but his assistants kept a good eye on me. The criterion for judging whether I was fit to go home was whether I was able to walk up two flights of the hospital stairs. I wasn't sure yet that my body could be trusted and it took me eight days to achieve that level of fitness and confidence. The heart wards are now in a new cardiac unit, but at that time they were in an old part of Bristol Royal Infirmary; but, cramped and old-fashioned as the accommodation seemed, there was a real pride in the doctors and nurses as to what new medical technology, highly skilled surgeons and committed care can provide for patients. It was the NHS showing itself to best advantage at a time of crisis.

Returning home brought both relief and fear. I was faced immediately with supporting Benedict, our older son, in an appeal about the marks in one of his A levels, and then in a wrangle with Trinity College Dublin about whether his three As would be sufficient to enable him to do the English degree there that was his first choice. It was good to know that even after surgery, and with a still fuzzy brain, I could play a useful role in family life.

It was also great to be back in my own bed and not eating hospital food. Familiar territory yes, but was I really ready to survive without the hospital staff and routines of care and checking? I came back laden with drugs – painkillers to help with the pain from the wound, a selection of tablets for blood pressure, and the need to have my warfarin level tested regularly and kept in the right balance. But the operation was over, I was told by doctors and nurses and by my own family that I was on the road to recovery and, as my confidence improved, gradually I could start to go out and meet people.

In practical terms one of the most significant parts of the recuperation process was when, after six or seven weeks, I joined a cardiac exercise class that took place twice a week in Wells Town Hall. Part of the class was given over to advice and discussion but before that, in each session, there was an exercise circuit that we all took part in – raising weights, step-ups, fast walking and so on. Age and fitness varied and we could take it at our own pace and level. The class ranged from the young and potentially active to the very infirm, and towards each other there was shared encouragement and human warmth. We were in this journey to health together. What was so good about this was that it made me push my body further than I would have done on my own, and so I came to realize that my heart was not about to give up on me and that I didn't need to be fearful of vigorous exercise.

But recovery wasn't all plain sailing. Having missed our summer holiday, we decided to go away at the end of October and booked a cottage in the East Neuk of Fife. I caught a bad cold which got no better during the two weeks. It was difficult for me to get about much and I didn't sleep well, with a lot of night sweats. On getting back home again I went to the doctor and was referred to a lung specialist. An X-ray showed that I had a lot of fluid in one lung. I was given antibiotics and a further appointment was arranged for two or three weeks' time. If nothing had shifted, I would be admitted to hospital. One of the side effects of taking warfarin is that you feel the cold much more acutely, which coupled with weakness after the operation and anaesthetic made me more vulnerable to infection. Anyway, to the specialist's surprise, when I had a second X-ray the fluid had cleared dramatically. At the same time as the antibiotics, a nutritionist had recommended that I take probiotic tablets to build up my resistance again. I continued taking them for a long time and still do through the winter months. I think that they helped my recovery substantially.

Another important step I took, with Cressida's encouragement and support, was to change my diet. We did not eat a lot of meat as two of our children were vegetarians at that time, but we made sure that if I did eat meat it was chicken. I started to eat more fish and reduced the amount of cheese that I ate (and loved). I also tried to cut back, not always successfully on snacks, cakes and chocolate.

By the end of 2008 I was beginning to be involved in Cathedral meetings again and resumed work fully in January 2009. I continued to take exercise, walking Toby, our black Labrador, each day, with occasional longer hikes on days off. Gradually I started to attend yoga classes again. By the summer of 2009 when we were on holiday in France I was swimming regularly and able to climb 2,000 – metre mountains, if more slowly than before. It felt that I had come a long way from the previous summer.

How have I changed through the experience of illness and recovery? I suppose that little by little I have learned to take better care of myself – to listen to my body when I am tired and to permit myself not to be so driven in my patterns of work.

I am more aware of the spiritual significance of my body, and that I am not just a mind or a spirit that can ignore physical disciplines in my relationship with God. Yoga has been important as a way of getting in touch with my body and cherishing the different parts of it. I have started to go for a massage once a month. I am trying to eat less and eat healthily. I have lost weight and continue to exercise – not that I was ever that large! At the same time, I have become more aware of my physical vulnerability. I listen to my body and especially my heart, for signs of malfunction. I am more realistic about the process of decay and ageing, and about the dangers of getting overstressed and overtired. But another aspect of my vulnerability is becoming conscious of my proneness to anxiety. This anxiety shows itself both by denial of my frailty by immersing myself in the busyness of my work, and by the opposite, a tendency to become neurotic and self-absorbed. I am more aware now that I am not all-powerful, and have a deeper realization that I offer what I can give in ministry out of my wounds as well as my natural gifts. The scar on my chest is a permanent reminder that I am called to a small share in the wounds of the Church, the body of Christ.

Some of the books that have been written out of a post-Jungian framework about men in mid-life discovering their woundedness, and accepting their shadow side, have been important to me.[120] I am quicker to recognize when my anger and stress levels are rising, and try to step back from situations and breathe deeply. When people are angry I try to see it as an issue for them, and not my own fault. I am no longer trapped by the reaction that I need to pacify them, or to make things better. This is a slow process of personal change in which both psychotherapy and silent prayer have played a significant part.

120 James Hollis, *The Middle Passage: From Misery to Meaning in Midlife*, Inner City Books, 1993; Robert Moore and Douglas Gillette, *Magician, Lover: Rediscovering the Archetypes of the Mature Masculine*, Harper Collins, 1991; Robert Bly, *Iron John*, Element Books, 1991.

The illness has also marked a transition in that I am much more aware that the time that remains for me is limited, both as I move towards retirement, and as the unknown day of death comes closer. I increasingly measure time from the end rather than the beginning of life.

Vulnerability has also influenced the kind of ministry I exercise. It has made me more alert to people's stories, to the pain and struggles that they face. Before the illness people already came to me for spiritual direction or accompaniment. I am able to listen to others, but I think that facing some of my own fears has made me more alert to the unspoken thoughts and fears that other people bring to me, and I hope has given me more compassion with their life journeys and searching after God. I was on prayer lists in many places. The prayer of others, of family, of friends, colleagues, my cell group, the congregations of the Cathedral, not least at the monthly healing service in the Lady Chapel, helped me through my illness – this is not something dramatic or easily explained – just a sense that my anxieties were being held and that others were willing me back to health, holding me before God as the source of all healing.

Now I find that I want to pray for others, to bring them into the love and light of God, especially those closest to me – my family, those who have entrusted me with their stories of faith, my cell group, my colleagues, and those who I know are in a particular time of crisis. I do not always find time to pray beyond the regular pattern of morning prayer and evensong in the Cathedral, but, at least in Wells, we try to lead these in a reflective and contemplative way, and the daily offices give time for me to remember. At other times I can pray in silence, and the first draft of this account of illness and recovery was written during twenty-five days of solitude in the western highlands of Scotland, an extended retreat, when there was time to rest, still the mind, and give myself to God.

Perhaps the sense that time is limited has also made me want to communicate what I have learned over the years about God. The theological project I started in the waiting period before the operation has continued with seven essays now written and in the process of being revised. The essays probe two significant contemporary writers on faith; one, a Jewish philosopher, Emmanuel Levinas,[121] and the other the Orthodox theologian, John Zizioulas.[122] Both writers speak of the otherness of God in ways that challenge the categories and expectation of western theology. They trace a journey from concern for the self towards the priority of responding to the other person, a journey that provides a framework for the healing of every soul. Both stress human embodiment and that the soul is healed only by aligning itself with God's love for the material world that he has created. I have found that even the body in illness can become an offering to the Other. In the experience of limitation, compassion and mercy can be called out from another person, whether family, friend or stranger. Such calling out of compassion gives a foretaste of the self-giving without reserve that Zizioulas describes as the communion of persons, communion that is constitutive of the life of God. In spite of the abstract nature of Levinas's and Zizioulas's thought this process of writing has been an intensely rewarding experience. It has made me work through a dialogue between the authors that has been going on in my head and heart for the past thirty years, a dialogue that has shaped my preaching and teaching.

Preaching has always been important in my ministry. It takes me time to prepare and write a sermon. In the Cathedral at the Eucharist and evensong I preach from a full typed – out script. There is a tradition at Wells of the congregation listening intently to the preacher, often asking for a copy of the sermon, and sometimes discussing what has been said. Such attentiveness demands discipline from the preacher in wrestling with scripture and trying to let the word of God be heard in the now of that particular service. Since my operation, I find that I speak

121 Emmanuel Levinas, *Totality and Infinity*, Duquesne University Press, 1999; Emmanuel Levinas, *Otherwise than Being*, Duquesne University Press, 1999.

122 John Zizioulas, *Being as Communion*, Darton, Longman and Todd, 2004; John Zizioulas, *Communion and Otherness*, Continuum, 2006.

more directly; the physical crisis I faced and the uncertainty I lived with, have made me more challenging in calling people to respond to God. I expect the sermon to be an occasion when hearts and minds are enlivened and prayer deepened. Preaching in Wells Cathedral is helped immensely by the beauty of the architecture and the power of the music. The dignity of the liturgical action makes the Cathedral a transforming space where people's faith can be nurtured and broadened.

Looking back over the past five years, I can see that much has changed in me, in my relationship with my family, and in the outworking of my faith and in the exercise of ministry. I am fortunate that medical technology has advanced and that the valve was able to be repaired. If the leak had happened thirty years ago I might well be dead by now. I am grateful for the support and care I received from many people, especially from Cressida, Ben, Edmund and Esther. The journey through illness into recovery has been one we have made together, albeit in different ways. It has rebalanced relationships, and brought a measure of healing to past hurts.

I now have a sense of having been given a new stretch of time. I don't know what the future will hold, but I want to offer what I can to God, and I want to enjoy the life that I have now. But I remain bemused by the time that I will never remember, the time when I was on the operating table and my life and death were in someone else's hands. It is a time of discontinuity when my heart and my life were held by the skill of a medical team. I suspect that for the rest of my life I will be marked by that physical de-centering, and will puzzle about decay, healing, the care of others, and the passing of time.

7

Looking at the Bronze Serpent

CHRISTOPHER COLLINGWOOD

A premonition

I can recall exactly the moment when I knew that something was seriously wrong. It was at the evening celebration of the Eucharist on the Tuesday before Advent Sunday in 1992. The Gospel reading on that occasion went as follows:

> When some were speaking about the temple, how it was adorned with beautiful stones and gifts dedicated to God, Jesus said, 'As for these things that you see, the days will come when not one stone will be left upon another; all will be thrown down.'
>
> They asked him, 'Teacher, when will this be, and what will be the sign that this is about to take place?' And he said, 'Beware that you are not led astray; for many will come in my name and say, "I am he!" and, "The time is near!" Do not go after them.'
>
> 'When you hear of wars and insurrections, do not be terrified; for these things must take place first, but the end will not follow immediately.' Then he said to them, 'Nation will rise against nation, and kingdom against kingdom; there will be great earthquakes, and in various places famines and plagues; and there will be dreadful portents and great signs from heaven.' (Luke 21.5–11)

As this was read, I had an utter conviction that it was about me personally; it seemed to speak directly to my condition. It was I, as it were, who was the temple, and it was all going to come tumbling down. It came to me as something of a premonition, the intuitive knowledge of something as yet to be confirmed by any medical evidence. By the following Saturday, however, the day before Advent Sunday, the day poised at the end of one liturgical year and the beginning of another, I was undoubtedly ill and could do no other than take to my bed.

In the days running up to that Tuesday it is true that I had not felt entirely well. I had been experiencing pains in my groin and in my testes. My wife had been keen that I see the doctor but I had ignored her concern. By the Wednesday morning, however, the pains were unmistakably there, especially in the testes, and I was persuaded that I should do something about it. As I described the symptoms to the doctor, I could see that my account was being taken with the utmost seriousness. He suggested that I might have an infection of the testes but spoke of having an ultrasound test to eliminate the possibility that it might be anything more serious. Needless to say, I was not a little alarmed and anxious at this point. Antibiotics were prescribed and the ultrasound test was delayed in order to give the medication a chance to work. In any case, the doctor wanted to be sure that even if the ultrasound test did show an infection, it did not hide something more sinister.

After a couple of days I began to feel somewhat better. I convinced myself that there was nothing seriously amiss at all. On the Saturday preceding Advent Sunday there was to be a big diocesan healing service in the church and I was very keen to be present. As the service began, I became aware that I had never before felt so disinclined to have anything to do with such a service. It was as if I was being faced with my own need and condition in such a way that I could not hide but I simply did not want to admit it. By the end I felt utterly exhausted and my colleagues persuaded me to go home to bed.

The reality of illness

The pain grew worse, extending now right down my legs with a burning sensation. I began to wonder whether I might have something like cancer, a prospect which filled me with sheer dread. My mental and spiritual state was by now becoming extremely fragile. I was moved to tears by the slightest thing and I felt a crushing sense of powerlessness and failure. From deep within, though, I heard the words being addressed to me: 'Follow me.' Within this experience of spiritual darkness I interpreted this to be an affirmation that I was loved by God, secure in God's love for me in Christ even if it turned out that I was terminally ill. For the most part, though, I wavered uneasily between anxiety and trust. I did not like being ill and I wanted to force the pace of recovery. When things did not improve, the possibility of a hospital admission was mentioned, and this scared me witless.

I had been Vicar of St Paul's, Bedford for just over two years. Having four young children meant that practically every bug going made its way into the home somehow, but in the immediate past I seemed to have had more than my fair share of viral infections. Just a couple of months previously, however, we had celebrated a major two-week-long festival in the church entitled *Through all the Changing Scenes of Life*. Its purpose had been to relate the Christian faith and the life of the church to the town-centre and civic institutions, to feed, stimulate and nurture those who already worshipped in the church, and to make connections with those who might have been considered, or who might have considered themselves, to be on the fringes of the church. There were all sorts of events that sought to engage people at practically every stage of their lives. It was the fruit of some eighteen months of preparation and organization not only by me but by a considerable number of other people, and it had been deemed by all involved to have been a resounding success. Without doubt, however, it had been hard work and I was exhausted. I found myself wondering whether the way that I was living my life might not, after all, have been very misaligned.

During the first few days of the illness I tried to persuade myself that it would be short-lived. Absurd though it seems now, I even held a staff meeting around my bedside. Furthermore, it felt entirely wrong that I should have taken to my bed during Advent, missing all sorts of things going on in the church and the parish, and the prospect of being incapacitated for Christmas was simply anathema to me. As the symptoms continued to get worse, though, it gradually dawned on me that I simply had to give in to the illness and let it take its course. It struck me that responding to the words, 'follow me', might have something to do with entering into the mystery of Christ's own suffering and death. Having held on – almost literally – for dear life, the decision to let go into the illness was felt at one level or another as something of a welcome relief. What began to emerge onto centre stage was a dawning awareness not so much of physical symptoms but of something far more mysterious and elusive.

A hereditary illness

All my life I had lived with the expectation that I would eventually succumb to an hereditary illness called Huntington's Chorea or, as it is now known, Huntington's Disease. This is a neurodegenerative disorder which seriously affects muscle co-ordination – hence the jerky, erratic movements of the limbs called chorea – and which leads to cognitive decline and dementia. My aunt and my two cousins had all died as a result of it at relatively early ages and the spectre of their illnesses and deaths hung over me like the sword of Damocles. I cannot remember a time when my aunt had not been hospitalized. My earliest memory of her goes back to when I can have been little more than five or six years of age. On this occasion, as on a few subsequent ones, she came to stay with her parents, my maternal grandparents, for the weekend. To a small boy she was a monster. Her speech was slurred and unintelligible, the movements of her limbs wayward and uncontrollable, and as we sat at the table to eat she slopped, dribbled and spilled her food all over the place. Whether I actually did this or just wanted to do it I cannot now remember but my memory persuades me that I hid cowering under the dining table, so afraid of her was I. The only shaft of light for me in this unremittingly gloomy picture came in the form of my father and grandfather cradling my aunt in their arms as they carried her to the toilet with immense gentleness and compassion. My aunt subsequently died in hospital at the age of forty-six when I was nine years of age.

My younger cousin Ann, older than I, was extraordinarily beautiful. When her first fiancé learned that the illness would almost certainly claim her, he decided that he could not go through with the marriage and we all felt intense sadness and disappointment. She did eventually marry someone else, but in her late twenties the tell-tale signs of Huntington's began to manifest themselves and she, too, was admitted into residential hospital care. My memory of the last time I saw her is of her as an untamed animal on all fours in the middle of her hospital room, her hair wild, and completely unreachable by any normal means of communication. She seemed to me to be utterly alone, locked in total inner isolation. She died at the age of thirty-six not long after I was ordained.

Ann's older brother, Brian, lived until he was forty-nine years old, having married and enjoyed something of a family life with his stepchildren. The marvel was that his wife embarked on the relationship knowing his condition full well. It seemed to me to be a relationship grounded in a remarkably generous love on her part. The disease, however, eventually took him too, although it remains unclear whether the circumstances of his death in a fire at his home suggested that it was truly an accident or whether he actually took his own life.

The illness which I experienced at the end of 1992 occurred sometime between the deaths of my two cousins. As I lay in bed, though, it was the awareness of Huntington's which began to fill my mind and occupy every waking moment. The reality of the disease had hung over our whole family from the beginning. Whenever we visited our grandparents its presence could be felt, either in the conversation about my absent aunt or in the physical symptoms which were beginning to be seen in my cousins, who lived with my grandparents. It was as if an awful darkness hung over all of us. It must have been a moment that my parents had been dreading when, my sister having manifested not dissimilar symptoms to Huntington's during her early teenage years, I articulated the question: 'Does Katharine have what Ann's got?' I cannot recall exactly how my parents reacted. I can only imagine that their worst fears and nightmares must have seemed to be coming true.

It was this question, however, which prompted my mother to mention the issue of Huntington's quite casually on one occasion to her own aunt. At this point an earth-shattering revelation was made. My mother's aunt informed her that there was absolutely no possibility of the illness coming down our side of the family. She was indeed stunned to discover that my mother did not know that her sister – my aunt and the mother of my two cousins – was not her full sister but in fact her half sister. The whole story then emerged that when my grandparents were engaged, my grandmother had actually been raped, thus causing her to conceive my aunt. Her parents had begged my grandfather to go through with the marriage to avoid the inevitable shame, and that indeed he did. The Huntington's, however, was clearly transmitted through the man who had committed the rape. There was no possibility that my mother could have been affected genetically in any way by the disease. I was eighteen years old when I discovered this.

The question may well be asked, though, as to how, if I knew beyond a shadow of a doubt that the disease could not be transmitted to me, I could have fallen ill thinking that it had something to do with Huntington's. The answer is fairly simple. Although I knew that I was untouched genetically by the disease, I had grown up with it as a pervasive presence to such an extent that *unconsciously* I had every expectation that my fate would be the same as that of my cousins and my aunt. This is what began to come into the full light of day as I reflected on my situation of being ill. I seriously thought that I might have been dying. While this might seem to any reasonable person to have been a ridiculous over-reaction, the physical symptoms were real. With hindsight, it became clear that the illness was psychosomatic and no satisfactory diagnosis of my physical condition was ever given. This is most emphatically not to say, though, that the illness was not real, rather that the nature of the illness was *psychological* in origin; that is to say, it was my *psyche* or soul which was diseased and the reality of the disorder was being manifested outwardly in *physical* symptoms.

The eruption of the unconscious

It was about two or three weeks after I first fell ill that the unconscious began to erupt. I became aware of a profound division within myself and I felt the pain that I had been carrying all my life in relation to Huntington's. It struck me with startling clarity that I was desperately afraid of death and that I was living my life in an attempt to cheat death itself, living at such a fast pace that I was seeking always to be one step ahead of it and out of its reach. I realized that I had spent my whole life with an unconscious expectation that I would die young and so I had to achieve something before it was too late. The force of the unconscious pushing itself into full consciousness made me aware that I was afraid of any really strong emotions, especially anger. Not only was Huntington's characterized by a gradual loss of control, it also manifested itself in the onset of aggressive and violent tendencies. My attitude to my own body, too, was one of suspicion and mistrust; I felt uncomfortable about my physical nature because the experience of Huntington's in the family had led me to believe that latent within the body were forces of destruction and disintegration.

The truth of all this self-knowledge led me to the conclusion at first that I was a complete sham and a fraud, that my whole life had been a lie. My priesthood felt hollow and the words addressed to Jesus, 'Physician, heal yourself' (Luke 4.23), seemed to be directed at me in a haunting and mocking way. How could I possibly minister to others when I knew myself to be so diseased and disordered? I felt exposed and vulnerable rather like the emperor without his clothes. I wondered whether everyone else had been able to see what I had failed to see all along. Yet at the same time, I was aware of a love upholding and enfolding me, sustaining me and guiding me through all this and, indeed, transforming me.

I began to talk about what I was going through with various visitors during this time, particularly with a priestly colleague in the parish, in whom I found a remarkable understanding, sympathy and acceptance. The more I allowed my unconscious to become conscious, the more the physical symptoms began little by little to disappear. I was not well enough to be in church for Christmas but I was able to take a service not long afterwards. I had been incapacitated for some five weeks in all, missing the whole season of Advent and most of Christmas. Never before, though, had the traditional Advent themes of death, judgement, heaven and hell, nor the Advent promise of God's coming among us to save, nor the reality of the birth of God in human form at Christmas, been so vivid and real for me. I had lived them during my illness.

A certain distance

It is now some twenty years since I went through this experience and some fifteen years since I first wrote about it.[123] Such a passage of time means that my memory of the actual events may not be reliable in every respect. The advantage, however, of distance from the actual experience itself allows the possibility of rather more mature reflection on its significance than was possible at the time, perhaps, in much the same way that we have

123 Christopher Collingwood, *The Divine Dance of Love: Sharing in the Mystery of Christ*, Canterbury Press, 1996, pp. 103–19.

come to understand that the Gospels, for example, are reflections several generations after the events associated with the life, death and resurrection of Jesus. Furthermore, the Gospels narrate not only the story of Jesus of Nazareth but also reveal something of the experiences, concerns and preoccupations of the communities in which they came to be written *in the light of* the experience of the first followers of Jesus. The reality of Christ is made flesh in our own lives and experiences, including – especially, perhaps – our experiences of illness and suffering. The Christ-event certainly illuminates our experience but so, too, does our experience inform and shape our knowledge and understanding of Christ himself. In my own case, the experience of illness in 1992 was not the end of it. There was undoubtedly a breakthrough at the time, but the coming into full consciousness of the unconscious can only happen gradually, otherwise we should be overwhelmed. While I have never experienced again the physical symptoms which I have described, or indeed anything approaching what might be called a psychosomatic illness, the reality of the way in which the awareness of Huntington's has shaped my life and experience has been an ever-present one – although to a much lesser extent now, perhaps – and there have been subsequent occasions when the unconscious has erupted with such force that I felt that I was indeed being completely overwhelmed.

There is, thus, a certain distance now from what I have related of the original experience, but there is an advantage in a degree of detachment: it allows, perhaps, a broader sense of perspective. In addition to this, there is my whole experience of life since then, in the light of which the original experience is seen to be part of an unfolding story. In order to explore the meaning of my illness and of its place in the development of who I am, I propose to consider it in relation to two passages of scripture. First, I should like to return to the extract from Luke's Gospel, which was quoted at the beginning of this chapter. Second, as a way of examining the nature and process of healing in relation to my experience from a slightly different perspective, I should like to look at that rather obscure story in the Book of Numbers about the serpent of bronze. I should then like to conclude the chapter by saying something about the implications of all this for one who is a priest.

The temple of the body

I suggested at the beginning that when I heard the reading about the destruction of the temple on that Tuesday evening, I felt that it was speaking directly to and about me. While this could be seen to be stretching a point somewhat, I do not believe that to be so. The story of the temple refers unequivocally to an actual historical building. At the same time, however, in the New Testament itself the temple is used as a metaphor both for Jesus in particular and for human beings in general. Towards the beginning of John's Gospel, for example, a connection is made between the temple and the body of Jesus:

> Jesus answered them, 'Destroy this temple, and in three days I will raise it up.' The Jews then said, 'This temple has been under construction for forty-six years, and will you raise it up in three days?' But he was speaking of the temple of his body. (John 2.19–21)

St Paul, too, speaks of the human physical body as the 'temple of the Holy Spirit within you' (1 Corinthians 6.19), and of the whole Body of Christ as the 'temple of the living God' (2 Corinthians 6.16). That the passage about the temple in Luke should have been applied to me personally seems not to be fanciful but to have something of a rationale in the scriptures themselves.

It may well be that at a deep level of the unconscious, beyond the ordinary processes of my rational mind, symbolic connections were being made between my body and the temple. Most significant of all, though, is that the passage in question is entirely apocalyptic in character, which is to say that it speaks of devastation, destruction and disaster in the context of the end times. At its root, however, an apocalypse is a revelation, an uncovering of something that is hidden, bringing it into the full light of consciousness. My experience was certainly of destruction of a kind and also of revelation. The real question, however, is what was being disclosed in and through it and why?

The drama of the self

In the twenty or so years that have passed since the illness, I have come to understand this largely through the practice of contemplative prayer – informed by my own Christian tradition – but also through the direct and personal encounter with the spiritual traditions of the East, largely that of Hinduism in India, but latterly through the practice of Zen – with its background in Buddhism – in this country. What I have come to see is that the core issue has to do with what might be called the drama of the self. For Christians, almost invariably, the primary and definitive question of life tends to be the one that Jesus himself asked of his first disciples: 'Who do you say that I am?'(Matthew 16.15; Mark 8.29; Luke 9.20). In the East, however, the most important question or at least the starting point, concerns not so much another person as oneself: 'Who am I?' The continual asking of this question of oneself was central to the method and practice of the great Hindu sage, Sri Ramana Maharshi. The purpose of asking the question again and again is that it should lead to Self-Realization. The radical questioning involved leads one beyond all partial realities and identities to the experiential reality of the Self, *Atman*, which is identical with the ultimate, with *Brahman* or God. This is exemplified in a conversation between Sri Ramana Maharshi (M) and a young man of twenty (D):

D: How to realize Self?

M: Whose Self? Find out.

D: Who am I?

M: Find it yourself.

D: I do not know.

M: Think. Who is it that says, 'I do not know?' What is not known? In that statement, who is the 'I'?

D: Somebody in me.

M: Who is the somebody? In whom?

D: May be some power.

M: Find it.

D: How to realize Brahman?

M: Without knowing the Self why do you seek to know Brahman?[124]

Zen begins in a similar place. Commenting on the ancient Chinese paintings known as the Ox-herding pictures, which have traditionally been understood to illustrate the spiritual development of a Zen student, Abbot John Daido Loori explains the importance of discerning whether a prospective student has the right motivation for beginning Zen training. With reference to the first one, entitled *The Search for the Ox*, he writes:

> Physical and psychological well-being are often by-products of this training, but if they are a student's main goal, there are more appropriate ways to work on them. But if the student is concerned with the ground of being, with fundamental

---

124 Sri Ramana Maharshi, *Talks with Sri Ramana Maharshi*, Sri Ramanasramam: Tiruvalannamai, 1996, pp. 60–1.

> questions of life and death – Who am I? What is truth? What is reality? What is life? What is death? – then they have come to the right place. Those are spiritual questions, and that is what Zen training is specifically designed to deal with. Those who begin Zen practice without an essentially spiritual motivation usually do not last long in the training . . . The ox depicted in K'uo-an's pictures represents the true self; thus the search is basically the search for the self, the nature of the self. The search commences the moment one raises the bodhi mind. The bodhi mind is the mind of enlightenment, the impulse and the aspiration for enlightenment, the aspiration to realize oneself.[125]

While the similarity between the Hindu and Buddhist perspectives may be readily appreciated, they might well seem to be a far cry from a Christian approach to anyone unfamiliar with such traditions. They can, however, be seen to complement one another and they meet in their understanding of what has been referred to above as the drama of the self. This is beautifully and archetypically illustrated in the myth of the Fall in Genesis 3. Writing out of his long and deep experience of living a contemplative Christian life in dialogue with the spiritual traditions of India, Bede Griffiths writes:

> The Fall is our fall into this present mode of consciousness, where everything is divided, centred on itself and set in conflict with others. The Fall is the fall into self-consciousness, that is into a consciousness that is centred in the self which has lost touch with the eternal Ground of consciousness, which is the true Self.[126]

Here is the essential drama of the self, played out as a conflict between a smaller, false or inauthentic self and a larger

125 John Daido Loori, *The Eight Gates of Zen*, Shambhala, 2002, p. 43.

126 Bede Griffiths, *Return to the Centre*, Fount, 1978, p. 28.

true Self, which these great spiritual traditions recognize in one way or another. Another writer, Aelred Graham, – like Bede Griffiths a Roman Catholic, Benedictine monk, but with a deep knowledge of Zen rather than Hinduism – is at one with Griffiths in his analysis of what he calls 'humanity's chief source of trouble':

> Deep distress inevitably occurs whenever we identify what may be called our true self (the 'I') with the assertive, separative ego (the often all too-demanding 'me'): when, in other words, we allow our lives to be immersed in a private sea of feelings, perceptions, desires and aversions, whether physical or mental. This can involve us in a kind of counterfeit self-awareness, so vivid that we may mistake its contents for our very being: all we are is what feel we are.[127]

The drama of the self arises because we live *as if the separative ego were the true self*. It is not that the ego *per se* is bad; we could not operate in the world without it. But we have to allow the true self to live through the ego, and God through the true self. When we make the ego the centre and measure of reality, though, everything goes awry. For in truth, in our essential nature, we are ultimately separate from nothing, neither from anyone or anything else in creation, nor from God. As the Apostle Paul puts it, writing rapturously from his own deep realization of this truth without doubt, 'I am convinced that neither death nor life, nor angels, nor rulers, nor things present, nor things to come, nor powers, nor height, nor depth, nor anything else in all creation, will be able to separate us from the love of God in Christ Jesus our Lord' (Romans 8.38–9). And it is worth noting that it was as the result of Paul's own resolution of the drama of the self, in which he was able to surrender his ego to the larger reality of the self, that he was able to affirm, 'I have been crucified with Christ; and it is no longer

127 Aelred Graham, *Zen Catholicism*, Crossroad, 1994, p. 25.

I who live, but it is Christ who lives in me' (Galatians 2.20). Paul's true self is none other than Christ himself.

If we are able to get through life without being bruised, hurt and wounded as a result of the drama of the self, we are not only fortunate but also most unusual. Nor, it also has to be said, are most of us likely to experience the drama in quite the stark way that Paul did. His experience, however, illustrates the central issue. His encounter with the risen Christ on the Damascus Road can be understood as involving the coming to full awareness of his own separative ego and its destructive power – all the more painful, since his ego was highly religious in character and identity – and surrendering it to his true self, his Christ-self. So strong and assertive was his ego that it separated him not only from anyone who was not a Jew but also, as he came to see, from God. For a while, everything in his life came tumbling down and he had to be remade in the truth. It was from the perspective of this remaking that he was able to say:

> From now on, therefore, we regard no one from a human point of view; even though we once knew Christ from a human point of view, we know him no longer in that way. So if anyone is in Christ, there is a new creation: everything old has passed away; see, everything has become new! (2 Corinthians 5.16–17)

Illness experienced as the drama of the self

It is in the light of the kind of things that I have said above that I have come to understand what I think was going on when I was ill. It was in the illness that the drama of the self was played out. I have already suggested that the physical symptoms of the illness were a manifestation at the level of the body of a deep dis-ease within me, and that it was through the illness that the unconscious was beginning to force itself into conscious awareness. The fact that it was painful at every level of my being was because I had so identified myself with my ego that I had kept hidden – and repressed, perhaps – deeply troubling aspects of my early experience, and of my larger and more expansive self. There are good and understandable reasons for this. I mentioned above that without an ego we should be unable to function in the world. It is by means of the ego that we are aware of ourselves as distinct personalities. It enables us to attend to detail, for example, and to perform daily tasks. But it also performs a vital role in protecting and defending us while necessary against harmful aspects of our experience and thus ensuring our self-preservation. Unless it did so, we should be overwhelmed, crushed and deprived of any capacity to function in everyday life. The time comes, however, when the way in which that vital task is being performed becomes wholly counter-productive, destructive and even harmful. At that point the true self begins to make itself felt more strongly and the ego is invited to surrender itself to the larger reality. This, I take it, is part of what is involved in Jesus' words:

> If any want to become my followers, let them deny themselves and take up their cross daily and follow me. For those who want to save their life will lose it, and those who lose their life for my sake will save it (Luke 9.23–4; cf Matthew 16.24–5; Mark 8.34–5).

As a small child, my ego had performed a necessary task in protecting me from the frightening aspects of Huntington's. The problem was that I was so identified with my limited ego that the results were pathological: I was living at too fast a pace, working too hard, afraid of my emotional nature, suspicious of my body, fearful of illness and death, and so on. These things had an ultimately crippling effect on the way that I lived my life. It was this that had to be addressed and owned.

This is why the Gospel reading on that Tuesday before Advent Sunday spoke to me so powerfully. I had erected an edifice of myself, which on the surface looked to me – and indeed to many other people – grand and beautiful. Like the temple, too, I was dedicated to God, but largely through my ego. Just as Jesus had warned his disciples that they could be led astray, at one level I was also deceived and led astray by my own ego into thinking that reality from the perspective of my ego was the whole story. The wars and insurrections to which Jesus referred were, in my case, within me in the form of the drama of the self being played out between my ego and my true self. Jesus encouraged his listeners, though, with the words that they should not be terrified, for these things have to take place. There are earthquakes and the like but these are the precursor to something creative and hopeful. And later on in the chapter, beyond what was included in that Gospel reading, Jesus affirms, 'When these things begin to take place, stand up and raise your heads, because your redemption is drawing near' (Luke 21.28).

None of this interpretation could I have given at the time of the illness itself; I have reflected on the meaning of the illness ever since. There is, however, one other aspect of the whole experience which I believe demands further exploration, for it surely will not have gone unnoticed that the growth in the direction of the true self came about precisely through the intensification of pain and suffering. It is here that the story of the serpent of bronze may be able to help.

The serpent of bronze

This rather perplexing story occurs in the Book of Numbers in the context of the people of Israel's wandering in the desert after the exodus from slavery in Egypt. Despite longing for freedom, they complain to Moses that they were actually better off in Egypt where at least they were fed. On account of their 'strong craving' (Numbers 11.4), God sends first manna and then quails for them to eat. Thereafter they complain again that they would rather have died in Egypt than endure the trials of the wilderness (Numbers 14.2), and as the story continues to unfold, it is affirmed that God is at work in all of this as God seeks to bring the people into the land that has been promised. In other words, God is inviting faith and trust in everything that happens, including, and especially, the difficult aspects of their experience.

The catalyst for the making of the bronze serpent is the people's impatience with God, as a result of articulating which to Moses God sends poisonous serpents which bite and cause many to die. This brings the people to their senses; they recognize that they have fallen short, and ask Moses to request that God take the serpents away. Moses is told to make a serpent of bronze and put it on a pole, with the intention that whenever someone is bitten by a serpent, they look at the serpent of bronze and live. This raises the baffling question: How can it be that looking at the very thing which threatens our existence itself be the instrument of the much-desired healing?

All of us experience pain and suffering in some way or another; it is simply an unavoidable fact of life. Most people experience minor illnesses during their lives at the very least. Even if we have managed to get through life without anything serious, the onset of old age almost invariably brings with it, for however brief a period, the gradual waning of faculties and powers, such that there can be physical, mental, emotional or spiritual distress. Not surprisingly, most of us flinch from such things and seek to avoid pain. This becomes pathological, however, when we refuse to face up to the reality of the situation, and this is where the story of the bronze serpent can be of some help. The instinctive reaction of the Israelites would have been to run from the poisonous serpents: they had the capacity to harm and kill after all. This is a natural human response. With the bronze serpent, however, they are being invited to face up to what they fear by looking it squarely in the eye. The story thus presents us with two vital aspects of our experience. First, there is the pain and suffering that result when we are threatened or indeed overcome by danger. The enjoyment of or desire for pain itself is simply masochistic, and it would seem thoroughly distasteful to think that such an attitude was encouraged by God. The desire on the part of the people, therefore, that Moses should 'pray to the Lord to take the serpents from us' is entirely understandable (Numbers 21.7).

On the other hand, the fact that the serpents were there in the first place is attributed to the fact that the people ignore and reject a crucial fact: the need to surrender themselves in faith and trust to God. In complaining to Moses, they distance themselves from the larger all-embracing reality of God. Put another way, their corporate, separative ego asserts itself over and against a more expansive consciousness, and the result is imbalance and disorder. There is no way, however that they can ultimately avoid facing the truth about themselves, but in so facing the truth there is inevitably pain and suffering. This would seem to be the purpose of the bronze serpent: to hold up a mirror, as it were, to the people, so that the truth of their spiritual condition could be revealed to them. And it is precisely in the *facing of the truth* that they are preserved from destruction, with one important caveat. If the bronze serpent represents to the people the truth about themselves, and if it is in looking at the serpent that they are healed, it is first and foremost the case that in looking at the serpent they also look in, through and beyond to God, who is the instigator of the whole process of healing. It is divine love that enables us to face the truth, and it is truth faced in love which is the beginning of healing.

It is almost ubiquitously the case that 'human kind cannot bear very much reality'[128] and the journey towards the truth is invariably painful. It is actually the avoidance of truth, though, which is the ultimate cause of our distress, and the journey into the truth which is the occasion of our deepest healing. The bronze serpent presents to all of us the challenge to see that whatever pain and suffering comes our way contains within it the summons to and the promise of wholeness. In my own case, the crucial thing was not so much facing the horror of Huntingdon's Disease itself – terrible though it is – although

128 T. S. Eliot, 'Four Quartets' ('East Coker'), in *Collected Poems 1909–1962*, Faber & Faber, new ed. 2002.

that was undoubtedly part of it, as coming to see the inadequacy of my own response to its presence in my family and the crippling effects of my own disordered attitudes and behaviour which resulted from it. I felt that my whole life had been built on falsehood – itself a somewhat distorted and exaggerated attitude, of course – but it left me feeling, as I have already mentioned, that my priesthood itself was hollow. In concluding this account, therefore, it seems appropriate to say something briefly about how I see this relating to my experience of being a priest.

Illness and being a priest

Notwithstanding the fact that the order of King Hezekiah to break into pieces the serpent of bronze (2 Kings 18.2) – which had subsequently been set up in the temple – suggests a degree of ambivalence to its existence and use within the Jewish tradition, it is also the case that the Gospel of John alludes to it in seeking to understand something of the mystery of Christ himself: 'And just as Moses lifted up the serpent in the wilderness, so must the Son of Man be lifted up, that whoever believes in him may have eternal life' (John 3.14). The implication here is that an understanding of the significance of the serpent of bronze will enable a deeper penetration into the meaning of what it is for Jesus to have been lifted up on the cross.

Paul articulated well the way in which the rational mind baulks at the suggestion that the cross is in some way a clue to the mystery and reality of God:

> Jews demand signs and Greeks desire wisdom, but we proclaim Christ crucified, a stumbling block to Jews and foolishness to Gentiles, but to those who are the called, both Jews and Greeks, Christ the power of God and the wisdom of God. For God's foolishness is wiser than human wisdom, and God's weakness is stronger than human strength. (1 Corinthians 1.22–5)

Just as the Israelites were invited to look at the bronze serpent in order to be healed, so, too, it is in contemplating Christ that the ultimate healing of all things is brought about. The cross presents us with the reality of the human condition in all its depth. Here, indeed, is the truth about ourselves in all our pain and suffering, but also the nature of divine love. What we see in Christ crucified is the very image of God and also a mirror reflecting us back to ourselves. In this sense, Christ becomes the true serpent of bronze, whose very wounding becomes the agent of healing, precisely because he is prepared to accept that wounding and enter into it to the full. Nor is it the case that the resurrection wipes all this away as if it were not real or did not really happen, for the risen Christ still bears the imprint of the nails and the spear in his risen body (John 20.27). The resurrection transforms us in such a way that everything that we have experienced contributes to who we are in the fullness of resurrection life.

Every human being has the vocation to enter into the mystery and reality of the death and resurrection of Christ as the path to the fullness of life, whether this is consciously recognized and acknowledged or not. For Christians, this is symbolized by receiving baptism and by sharing in the Eucharist, and in this regard the ordained priest is no different. Part of the particular vocation of the ordained priest, however, is to hold up to the whole Church and beyond the reality of Christ, not in such a way that makes this exclusive to the ordained priesthood, but in a manner that the universality of the calling to embody Christ is recognized and acted on by all. In this sense, the ordained priest is called to be a visible sign. And if the vocation of the ordained priest is to embody for all something of Christ in his death and resurrection, then part of that embodying will include the suffering and pain that comes from being wounded – not least through illness – simply as part of the whole human condition in which all humanity shares, as well as the transformation that arises when we dare to face it in all truth and honesty with the help of God's grace and love, and begin to know the resurrection life for ourselves. The ministry to which we are called is not primarily ours, of course, but that of Christ himself. The task of the ordained priest, like that of all Christians, is to 'present' Christ, or better, perhaps, to allow Christ to be presented, in all that we are and do, a presentation which is thoroughly eucharistic in character and shape. And, if Christ is to be presented authentically, this necessarily includes the shadow aspects of our lives – so that when others look at us, they see through us to Christ himself. This is no cause for self-elevation or self-aggrandisement. That would be precisely to 'fall into self-consciousness, that is into a consciousness that is centred in the self which has lost touch with the eternal Ground of consciousness, which is the true Self'.[129] Rather, it is to affirm with Paul that if we must boast, we will boast of the things that show our weakness (2 Corinthians 11.30). The ordained priest, like every other human being, is weak, frail, fragile, vulnerable and wounded – in other words, sick – and it is part of the sheer mystery of our life in God that it is when we face and own this truth for ourselves, that Christ, our true self, is uncovered and begins to live fully from the very depths of our being, where he is present already, and has been from the very beginning, and healing begins for our sake and for the sake of all.

129 Griffiths, *Return to the Centre* (see p. 104).

8

In God I put my Trust

JANE KENCHINGTON

Discovery

Friday 25 April 2008 began as a day of celebration. It was the twelfth birthday of Sarah, our younger daughter; I had just turned fifty the previous day. And it was my day off. By 7.50am on that day, my mood had changed. As I stood in the hallway, still in my night dress, seeing both our daughters off to school, I happened to brush my hand across my chest and I felt a lump. I immediately thought, 'This could be cancer!' I calmly told Richard, my husband, who felt the lump as well – yes, there was something there. I phoned the doctors' surgery for an appointment that morning.

I was no stranger to cancer: my sister, Catherine, had had breast cancer only two years previously. At that time, I had tried to find out as much as I could about the disease. Catherine had survived thus far. Thinking of incidents much earlier on in my life, I could only remember people who had died from cancer. Indeed, as a child, I grew up thinking that if you suffered from cancer, it was equivalent to being given a death sentence. But I did know that treatment over the years had improved significantly; and while one might dread cancer, survival rates are much higher – at least for some cancers.

Things moved fast. I saw my GP that morning and she referred me to the local hospital. The hospital responded by offering me a 'One Stop' appointment twelve days later in which diagnosis would be confirmed there and then.

I was in limbo. Whom should we tell? We decided not to talk to our daughters about it at this stage – what was the point of letting them worry in case the lump was benign? So Richard and I decided that we would wait to inform people (or not) until we knew for certain. I tried to continue as if nothing was wrong. Meanwhile, the lump began to feel harder, even though it was small.

The day of the hospital appointment arrived. I had decided that, since it would mean sitting around for three hours in various waiting rooms, I'd be better going on my own. I did not want Richard becoming stressed and anxious as we waited to see medical staff: it would be hard enough coping with my own emotions. Besides, I had plenty of reading to do in preparation for a course that I was booked to go on for the whole of the following week. So I went alone to the hospital, armed with my basket of papers to read and I sat through the waiting periods between the various people I had to see, busily reading and trying to concentrate. Around me, women were emerging from consultations, in tears. Those waiting rooms were not easy places.

My first appointment of the afternoon was with the breast cancer consultant who proceeded to do an ultrasound scan of my breasts. I asked him right at the start to show me the screen and point out what he could see because I was genuinely interested. He pointed out benign cysts and then came to *the* lump. It looked different from the benign cysts and I remember saying to him, 'It's cancer, isn't it?' He clearly did not want to commit himself at that stage. He changed the subject, asking me what I did. When he discovered that I was a priest, he told me that his mother had been a secretary to the late Bishop Leslie Brown – whom I had met while at theological college. He then told me that Bishop Leslie had confirmed him. I felt a moment of consolation. It felt that God was with me in this place. After a mammogram, I was sent back to the Consultant for the results. Yes, it was cancer. No, I would not need a mastectomy. How about coming in for day surgery a fortnight later? I was relieved that I did not have to change my work plans. I felt a sense of calm: so be it. I was then handed over to a cancer care nurse for a 'chat'. She was surprised that I was on my own and that I seemed quite calm. I explained to her that I understood that this particular cancer, if caught early enough, was curable. She conceded that I was correct. What I did not tell her was that I knew that when I got home I would be e-mailing my colleagues and friends, asking them to pray for me/us.

Telling my family was the next step. Richard put his head in his hands; Lizzie (fifteen) burst into tears; Sarah (twelve) was more sanguine. It was at that point that I realized that I would need to be even more lovingly supportive of them than I might normally be – and offer them hope. I would need to be careful as to what extent I shared any fears I might have with them, at least in these early days. I needed them to be strong for and with me – which they proved to be. I could not cope with this if my nearest and dearest were going to pieces. I had come to realize through accompanying my sister through her illness that it was far harder being the accompanier than the patient. In accompanying someone who has a critical illness, you can feel completely powerless. You see the person suffering, you dread the fact that they might never recover and you feel impotent – you are not in control. When I was the patient, I still felt some element of control, even though theologically, I was deluding myself!

Then out of the blue, Alison, a long-standing friend, who lives miles away, phoned me that evening. She was totally oblivious to what was happening; it was as if God had sent me an angel. When praying Compline that evening, the words of Psalm 91 (CW) spoke to me: 'Whoever dwells in the shelter of the Most High and abides under the shadow of the Almighty, shall say to the Lord, "My refuge and my stronghold, my God, in whom I put my trust."' The first of a series of inspiring, wonderfully comforting pieces of scripture, always appropriate to how I felt on a particular day, spoke to me.

Does God answer prayer?

Coming to terms with the fact I had cancer, raised all sorts of memories and questions. I could remember when a lovely young woman, who was a Christian and a wife and mother was diagnosed with breast cancer. She was one of those people who 'shone'. The church prayed for her healing. After many months of fighting the disease, she died, leaving two boys under the age of three and a distraught husband. Then there was David Watson, the Christian evangelist. At the time, I was worshipping in an open evangelical Anglican church and many people believed that, if there were enough people praying for David, God would heal him and restore him to full earthly health. People world-wide prayed for David's healing. David died at the age of fifty-seven. This shook some of the Christians I had met through this church. 'We prayed to God and God did not heal him. What has gone wrong?' I had not encountered this theology before. I had believed healing was in God's hands and one just had to offer it to God and accept what would happen; God healed sometimes and not at other times. I had to accept that there was the element of mystery. The degree of faithfulness did not seem, necessarily, to equate with the type of outcome.

But the question remains. What are we doing when we pray for healing? Jesus says, 'I will do whatever you ask in my name, so that the Father may be glorified in the Son. If in my name you ask me for anything, I will do it' (John 14.13–14). How does one make sense of this when people pray for sick people and sometimes they die and yet in other instances they recover? Humankind cannot rationalize about healing except that it appears that it is not for us to know. God knows our needs before we even ask him and God supplies our needs because God loves us. And yet there is a clear imperative for us to ask God for things in Jesus' name and believe God will grant it.

> God nowhere guarantees us freedom from misfortune and suffering and certainly not from death. But God knows that the greatest good He can give us is the ability to trust Him not to let us down in the final resort by raising us to new life . . . One of the important ways in which God gives us new life is by our asking God for things, because in doing that we get to know God better and ourselves better.[130]

What do we mean when we talk about Christian healing? 'Christian healing is, first and foremost about Christ . . . It is the whole work of Christ, in a person's body, mind and spirit, designed to bring that person to that wholeness which is God's will for us all.'[131] Martin Israel emphasized that 'healing is the process whereby humanity is gradually restored to the divine image in which it was created so that we all can come to share in the very being of God . . . full healing involves more than a surface amelioration of suffering, essential as this may be in the short term.'[132] Becoming whole is more than a life-time's journey: it is about the emergence of our true selves; the integration of those parts of us that seem to war against each other that St Paul describes so well.[133] So when we pray for healing, we are praying that the person concerned is made whole in body, mind and spirit – that a greater integration may take place and a more Christ-like character will emerge. We believe that God's greatest desire is for us to draw closer to God, which may include a sharing

130 H. A. Williams, *Becoming what I am*, Darton, Longman and Todd, 1977, pp. 48–9.

131 Morris Maddocks, *Twenty Questions about Healing*, SPCK, 1981, p. 7.

132 Martin Israel, *The Quest for Wholeness*, Darton, Longman and Todd, 1989, p. 1.

133 Romans 7.15, 7.24–5: 'I do not understand my own actions. For I do not do what I want, but do the very thing I hate . . . wretched man that I am! Who will rescue me from this body of death? Thanks be to God through Jesus Christ our Lord!'

in the sufferings of Christ.[134] If, perhaps, in praying for healing, the person concerned becomes more Christ-like, this is an instance when God's glory may be seen through that sick person.

Coming to terms with cancer

The day after I had been diagnosed with cancer, I returned to the hospital for the pre-operation procedures. I played hymns in the car throughout the journeys and I found myself crying. I did not want Lizzie and Sarah to lose a mother while they were so young. 'Please God, just give me a few more years,' I found myself praying. I do not think I was crying for myself: deep down I had a trust that everything would be alright. The *fear* of dying did not really haunt me at all, but I did not want to leave my loved ones. The diagnosis had made me face my mortality. When one is well, one does not give much thought to death; now I was facing my own mortality. I knew many women get this disease (one in nine women will contract breast cancer) yet many women survive for several years after the treatment.

People phoned and e-mailed. I was told that I was allowed to cry . . . even though most of the time I didn't feel like crying at all. I was sent some words of Julian of Norwich, reminding me that, despite the tempests that hit us, God will not allow us to be overcome.

Working took my mind off the diagnosis. I found myself operating on two levels. On one level, I was preaching and presiding at services, seeing people, attending meetings and acting as if nothing was amiss; on another, deeper level, I had emotions fermenting inside me which I poured out in prayer to God/Christ and wrote in my spiritual journal. Instinctively and rationally, it did not occur to me to allow much of my emotional life to impact on what I was doing professionally.

---

134 *A Time to Heal – A Report for the House of Bishops on the Healing Ministry*, Church House Publishing, 2000, p. 14.

I was there to serve others, not to inflict my troubles on them. To put it bluntly, it would be 'business as usual', as I informed my colleagues in the e-mail I sent them asking for their prayers. No other option even occurred to me. It was much more to do with appearing to be 'strong' – which is no doubt associated with my formation as a child and young adult. Being an ordained woman in the Church during the years when there was so much opposition to the ordination of women left me with no option than to be strong. Appearing to be strong was not a mechanism of denial. Privately, I was certainly facing the possibility of death.

I continued to pray the Daily Office and regularly found scripture speaking to me in what seemed to be God-incidental ways. 'The Lord is my light and my salvation; whom then shall I fear? The Lord is the strength of my life; of whom then shall I be afraid?' (Psalm 27 CW). Exactly. 'Hold onto it,' I told myself. It was a psalm that Bishop Leslie Brown had quoted when I was at theological college. Now here it was again, offering me comfort. On another day, I awoke feeling rather low. Again a set psalm spoke directly into my heart. 'Why are you so full of heaviness, O my soul, and why are you so disquieted within me? O put your trust in God; for I will yet give him thanks, who is the help of my countenance, and my God' (Psalm 42 CW). I was to discover that time and time again, throughout this illness, scripture upheld me.

For the most part, the 'two level' strategy worked . . . until four days before my operation, when the enormity of it all threatened to overwhelm me and I could no longer keep the two levels separate. At this point, I was away from home attending a course on Conflict Resolution. In one way this was a good thing because it occupied my mind. On that particular day, I wrote the following in my prayer journal:

> For days I have felt stuff inside me that is ready to be born, and yet remains, to some extent, inarticulate. Fifty years old and I discover this. I have lived for fifty years – it seems like a

pivotal moment in my life. How do I determine to live the next fifty or less years left to me – if I am given that time?

O God – I want to live. The world is too beautiful to leave; I want to be with Richard – I love him dearly. I want the girls to have a mother accompanying them/being accessible to them for many more years. I do not want them to be motherless at this time in their lives. Jobs and ambition fade away into insignificance. What have you given me/made me to be that you want me to do/be for your glory? That is what I want – help me to discern that in these coming weeks as I convalesce. Lead me in your ways, lead me in your righteousness, lead me for your name's sake.

This is why I have not written up this journal: writing taps into my emotions and as long as I can keep a lid on them, I can cope with what's going on around me. I feel churned up now . . . I have got to face another day and a half of training. Please help me, Lord – give me the strength I need. Into your hands, I commend my spirit.

After that outpouring, my two levels of operation became increasingly harder to sustain. Rationality seemed to fly out of the window. I was supposed to take two services on the following Sunday and I knew I couldn't do it. The Archdeacon took over.

The day before I was admitted to hospital, Bishop John offered to anoint me and pray for me after a service in the cathedral. A small group of clergy gathered with him in the Galilee Chapel while he ministered. I felt safe here and 'held'. I was exceedingly grateful that there were many people praying, loving and supporting us.

Treatment

The day of the operation dawned. '*The* Day', I wrote in my journal. And, 'God, please support Richard, Lizzie and Sarah today.' Again scripture spoke to me as I prayed Morning Prayer: 'He asked you for life and you gave it to him' (Psalm 21 CW).

'We know that if the earthly tent we live in is destroyed, we have a building from God, a house not made with hands, eternal in the heavens. For in this tent we groan, longing to be clothed with our heavenly dwelling . . . For while we are still in this tent, we groan under our burden . . . we make it our aim to please him' (2 Corinthians 5.1–2, 4a, 9b). I wrote in my journal:

> Yes, my body's burden today is cancer and I pray that the operating surgeon will attack it and successfully remove it. Yes, I want to live! Yes, I want to please God. And then I found myself singing (and I could not stop), 'Fill thou my life, O Lord, with praise . . . that all my being may speak of your love.' That is what I truly want.

The rest of that day was spent travelling to the hospital; having surgery and waking up crying; returning to the day ward (I was expected to go home at the end of the same day); becoming increasingly more unwell (internal bleeding had started and would not stop), medical staff deciding that I had to have further surgery and admitting me to one of the main wards of the hospital. Once on the main ward, Richard (who had come to the hospital expecting to take me home) had to leave me again. I was told that the operation would take place any time from 11pm – depending on how busy the night surgeon was. The ward was noisy with people yelling in pain. Time seemed to stand still. I remember reading every page of the newspaper in between praying Evening Prayer and Compline. Prayer and set prayers and the lectionary were like anchors for me. I just held onto God. God gave me life and hope. God was my loving parent whom I believed was holding me. In God I rested. It was unthinkable to do or think anything else. When Jesus asked the disciples if they wanted to leave him, as his teaching was proving difficult to accept, Peter replied, 'Lord, to whom can we go? You have the words of eternal life. We have come to believe and know that you are the Holy One of God' (John 6.68–9).

At 2.30am, they collected me and wheeled me back to the operating theatre. At 3.30am, I awoke in the recovery room, crying. I do not know why I was crying – it might have been from relief, it might have been the effect of the anaesthetic. The nurse was kind. I was then returned to the noisy ward where I spent the rest of the night awake, watching the clock's hands moving exceedingly slowly. By 6am, I was praying Morning Prayer – again, it was a life-line for me. Fortunately, I was allowed to return home at the end of that day and it was a huge relief to be back with my family and in a comfortable bed.

A few days later, I returned to the hospital to be told the results of the operation and be advised about the next stage of treatment. The key information was that the cancer had not spread – no cancer cells had been found in the lymph nodes. But the cancer that they had removed was a grade 3 type – the most aggressive type of cancer. If I had radiotherapy and took the drug tamoxifen for five years, statistically, there was a ninety-three per cent chance of the cancer not returning in the next ten years. That was encouraging.

Journey to recovery

On returning home, I had post-operative pain to cope with. No pain killers seemed to work. For several days, prayer was snatched. I tried to pray the set psalms and readings of each day. I slept little and cried a lot. I cried when I went to see the GP; I cried when blood samples were taken; I seemed to cry a lot of the time in the first few weeks after the surgery. I felt so drained and tired and yet couldn't sleep because of the pain. It really seemed a low point. It was not that I was angry with God; it was not that I was frightened. Perhaps all the emotions that had been building up over the past month were being released. Yet, at the same time, I felt an invisible support surrounding me through other people praying for me.

I wrote in my journal, 'Thank you, Lord. Please heal me; give me patience; take away this pain; lift my mood – I feel so "down".'

As the time progressed, I clung onto my pattern of praying the Offices and reading scripture. It was also at this time that

I decided to read *Enduring Melody*.[135] I have found Michael Mayne's books to contain gems of theological insight and I expected this book to be of great help to me. My journal became peppered with quotes from his book and enabled me to ponder things deeply in my heart. I thought about what *Cantus firmus*[136] became rooted and gradually developed through my childhood experience of church. I continually looked back with a great sense of gratitude for all that had been: how faith in Jesus Christ had been nurtured; how I could trace God's hand on my life over the years; how much I had been blessed by the many people I had encountered in the last fifty years. Beneath all the pain, there were feelings of thankfulness and a deep trust in God; there was nowhere else I could place my trust and through this came a deep sense of joy and peace.

Richard, Lizzie and Sarah were great supports to me, treating me kindly, with patience and love. Fortunately, Richard worked from home, and managed skilfully and lovingly, to be available to me when I needed him but also sensitively gave me space to rest, read and pray. After the initial shock, Richard adopted a rational approach to my illness, which enabled him to give Lizzie the support she needed. Sarah's coping mechanism was to talk to school friends whom she describes as being 'rocks' for her through this time.

I needed corporate worship as well and, by the beginning of June, I had enough energy to walk the short distance to the local church to attend the Sunday Eucharist. Once more I was fed. We sang two hymns that had been significant to me during this period of illness: 'Fill thou my life' (which I'd sung on the day of my surgery) and 'All my hope on God is founded' – a hymn I had played repeatedly in the car as I travelled to and from the hospital. We sang Psalm 46 (CW), 'God is our refuge and strength, a very

---

135 Michael Mayne, *Enduring Melody*, Darton, Longman and Todd, 2006.

136 Mayne, *Enduring Melody*, pp. 1 ff. Mayne likens the *cantus firmus* to the 'ground bass' or the firm ground of our lives. It comprises certain critical truths and experiences that have seized and shaped a person and which lie at the deep centre of the person.

present help in trouble. The God of hosts is with us; the God of Jacob is our stronghold.' These God-incidences reminded me of Psalm 139 (CW), 'Where can I go from your spirit? Or where can I flee from your presence?' God was there with us.

Since this time, I have met people who, on being diagnosed with a critical illness, stop going to church. I try to understand their reasoning, but worshipping with a group of Christians was essential for me during my illness. I needed to be part of the worshipping body of the Church: I might not have done very much, but I was able to 'be' and rest in God, upheld by the prayers of others. The hardest thing I found about going to church was tolerating trivial chatter from people in their avoidance of referring to my illness. For me, this illness had brought deep spiritual insights and there were precious few opportunities to even begin to share them. It made me reflect on how I would do sick visiting in the future; how I might give people the space to talk on a spiritual level. It made me question how we nurture people's faith so that, if critical illness strikes, they may have the wherewithal to move beyond the bewilderment, resentment, fear or anger that might result from a diagnosis.

The diagnosis of cancer made me question my lifestyle. Were there factors that contributed to it developing in the first place? Apparently, obesity, lack of exercise, alcohol consumption and a poor diet could be contributing factors. I did not think they applied to me. The medical staff I spoke to were non-committal. 'Just eat things in moderation', I was told. I was not convinced. Such was my determination to live, I kept thinking, 'What can I do to try to prevent this happening again? Why is it so common? There must be something!' I read avidly and I learned that diet played a role in keeping the body's immune system in condition. Stress depresses the immune system, so learning to manage stress levels seemed to be very important. I do not know if the changes I set out to make will do anything positive except to make me feel fitter, but focusing on this while I was in recovery provided me with something positive to do. I no longer felt so powerless. I wanted to stop it happening again. Was that because I was frightened of death? I do not think so. Someone wrote saying that they imagined that this cancer was a 'cruel blow'. That was not how I saw it most of the time. It was more a 'wake-up' call and a gift. In suffering, there can be a stripping, a purification of desires as one comes to see that the most important thing is to know Jesus Christ. In my own case, I kept throwing myself onto the mercy of God. There was no one else I could turn to. The cancer made me ask questions like, 'What is the most important thing in my life? How am I going to live the rest of my life, if I am given time?' It came down to my relationship with God and Christ. I found myself asking God to rescue me from wrongful desires: I longed to desire what God longed for me to desire. And I reached the point where I could echo St Paul's words, 'I want to know Christ and the power of his resurrection and the sharing of his sufferings by becoming like him in his death, if somehow I might attain the resurrection from the dead' (Philippians 3.10–11). Faith means, 'We do not live to ourselves, and we do not die to ourselves. If we live, we live to the Lord, and if we die, we die to the Lord; so whether we live or whether we die, we are the Lord's' (Romans 14.7–8). That, I came to realize, was all that mattered.

It made me look at my life and my lifestyle, address stress levels and exercise. Cancer had driven me into the hands of God in a powerful way. Things could never be the same again. Michael Mayne quoted from George Eliot's *Adam Bede*, 'It would be a poor result of all our anguish and our wrestling if we won nothing but our old selves at the end of it . . . Let us rather be thankful that our sorrow lives in us as an indestructible source, only changing its form, as forces do, and passing from pain into sympathy – the one poor word which includes our best insights and our best love.'[137]

Where now?

I was warned that the radiotherapy would leave me very tired and I was also told that I would not feel 'back to normal' for

137 Mayne, *Enduring Melody*, pp. xix–xx.

about twelve months. In the September, four months after surgery, I was out walking with friend Alison and found myself crying. I think it was brought about by the continued pain that caused sleep deprivation; by my wondering if I would ever feel fully well again; but also because I was living with a tension. Professionally, it felt that my colleagues (in their eagerness to welcome me back from sick-leave and affirm me) were encouraging me to return to things as they had been before May. It was a good intention. Yet I knew that I would not be returning as the same person and I was bewildered in discerning where God was leading me. God always calls us forward, not backwards. 'All' I wanted was to walk in a way of holiness, where motherhood, marriage and priesthood were in a better balance. I would ask myself the question, 'If I knew I had only twelve months left, how would I spend those months?' And I knew the answer would not be that of killing myself working at the expense of home life and health. I felt the pull to a more contemplative life, yet I was a priest in the Institutional Church where clergy very often work over sixty hours per week. As the autumn progressed, I felt as if I was thirty-nine weeks pregnant. Increasingly, I felt there was something in me that was preparing to be born. God was preparing me for something. On retreat later in November, I found myself deeply moved by the conclusion that perhaps God had allowed this cancer to develop to make me review how I was living my life. It truly was a gift to me. God gives us life and I wanted to know that quality of life 'and have it abundantly' (John 10.10). What ultimately mattered was to know Christ. Everything else was just not important.

Where did I go from here? I believe that no experience we undergo is wasted, provided we learn from it. Something good comes out of it, even though we may not perceive it for years. In one way, experiencing this illness was not something I would gladly embrace. On the other hand, however, had I not been ill, I would not have encountered God/Jesus in the way I did. The experience was bitter-sweet.

Sixteen months after my surgery, I was licensed to be Rector of a multi-parish Benefice. I have always been open about my history of cancer. Since arriving here, I have accompanied many sick people – some to their deaths. Michael Mayne wrote, 'I believe that one of the ways in which God can use our experience of darkness is to increase our imaginative understanding, reaching out to one another with love because we have been there too.'[138] There have been several incidences of cancer, including the tragic death of a twenty-year-old lad. This particular death presented me with the task of trying to help people through the theological minefield of God not seeming to answer their prayers. People seem to appreciate the fact that I have been on a cancer journey myself: it helps them to feel that I have *some* understanding of their plight. If that has been part of the gift that my experience of cancer has brought, then praise be to God.

Michael Mayne concluded, 'To die with gratitude for all that has been, without resentment for what you are going through, and with openness towards the future, is the greatest gift we can leave those who love us and who are left behind.'[139] I would like to change that to say that my hope is that, through this experience, I can live with gratitude for all that has been, without resentment for what I am going through, and with openness towards the future.

138 Mayne, *Enduring Melody*, p. xx.
139 Mayne, *Enduring Melody*, pp. 250–1.

9

Invisible Pain

KEVIN ELLIS

In torment, proving the fallacy of the impassible reminding him of omnipotence's limits[140]

Childlessness is a curious thing; it is something that is at one and the same time very public, yet very private. Most of us will know couples or individuals who do not have children. Priests and ministers will be able to name them as they think of people within their congregations. It is therefore a very public state of affairs. However, the reasons why people might be childless are multifarious: couples can make a choice not to have children. Whatever the reasons for that choice, it will have been well thought out, and such couples are often inaccurately labelled as 'selfish'. That will be a cause of unwarranted and unnecessary pain. This reflection is not written from a perspective of choosing to be childless. There will be people who seem not to have children; but whose children may have died, during gestation, at birth, as children, or as adults. As someone who has been involved in conducting funerals and dealing with the parents involved, I know that this is a source of unimaginable grief. Again, this lies outside of the scope of this present theological narrative. I write from the perspective of someone who would love to have had 'birth' children; but was unable to do so because of male infertility. This is something I have written about previously, but under the general guise as a

140 R. S. Thomas, 'Crucifixion', *Counterpoint*, Bloodaxe Books, 1990, p. 36.

'call to arms' for the church to take seriously the curse of childlessness.[141] Writing a personal reflection about the pain of childlessness is something that I have always been hesitant about for several reasons. Firstly, the pain or dance with childlessness can be unending; therefore this offering is an incarnation that is fixed at this particular point in time.

As an aside, it is important for readers to understand why I choose to use the imagery of dance to describe my relationship with childlessness. Dance, firstly, can with it capture an emotion of sadness and gladness. Secondly, a movement can be individual or with another and others; intuitive or choreographed. Thirdly, and I draw here upon the medieval *Le Dance Macabre* (Dance with Death) to make the point, just as our human companions, at one time, were aware that they always danced with mortality; as some other writers in this volume may indicate. For those who are childless, childlessness is always present; it never fully disappears; like the childhood monster in the room; it is always at the very corner of the eye. Fourthly, as the early Eastern theologians understood, the relationship that may exist within the triune God of the Christian faith can be described in terms of a dance.

Secondly another reason for my hesitancy is that male infertility is not usually spoken about; it is hidden. This is despite some of the statistics. Male infertility and subfertility are not uncommon. In the UK, 2.3 million men acknowledge that they suffer from some form of erectile dysfunction. In thirty per cent of cases the reason a couple cannot conceive is to do with the male, although there is evidence that in up to fifty per cent of cases, male infertility is a contributing factor.[142] Thirdly, for some childless couples, because I am adoptive parent I lose the right to speak about childlessness. While I adore my adoptive son and would do anything within my power for him without

141 Kevin Ellis, *Christianity and Childlessness*, Grove Books, 2006.

142 'ABC of Subfertility: Male Subfertility', *British Medical Journal*, 20 September 2003, Vol. 27, p. 669.

a moment's thought, I am still infertile; I am then a curious phenomenon, a childless father. Fourthly, to reflect theologically on my story would involve a collision with the world of the scriptures, which contain little positive about the predicament of those who long for children; and yet are unable to have them. It is for this reason that I begin with the story of another.

> She stood in the shadows watching him. She had heard much about him – not that people had spoken directly to her, they never did. Now she saw him in the flesh she was not sure, but she had come so far. She had come far not just in terms of geography.
>
> For years she had hidden on the edge of her society. Theresa had brought shame on her family: she was not able to find a husband and found herself cut off from the worship of her people. Theresa had a constant flow of blood. People muttered when they saw her. 'Poor Theresa' was the best she could hope for. But she was here now with him, this Galilean teacher.
>
> Theresa did not want people to know, for she had spent a lifetime cultivating invisibility. If only she could touch the hem of his garments, things would be different. She reached out her fingers tingling as they felt the cloth. Power flowed into her: and she felt nothing for the first time since she could remember.
>
> Then the teacher turned, and he knew. He asked and she stammered forward. He smiled instantly and after a while, almost as if she had forgotten how to, so did Theresa. She was free to do so many things; but it was too late for her to fulfil some of the dreams she had had: having children probably being one of them.

The above narrative based on Mark 5.25–34 is an example of hidden childlessness, the woman with the haemorrhage would have been unable to have children. She presumably was childless because of her medical condition, but her condition was exacerbated by religious tradition. While it is true that her issue of blood would have excluded her from the worship of Israel's God; her lack of children would have contributed to her shame and, as we shall see, to a feeling of worthlessness about her role in her family and society.

There are strange commonalities, as well as differences, between the story of Theresa and my own. We are separated by two millennia, yet snared by a similar narrative that involves a lack of children. We are from different cultures: She was, I imagine, a Jewish Palestinian woman; I am a male Church of England priest. Yet, both of us would wrestle with a faith tradition in which children are a gift and blessing, an act of grace. She presumably would never have been married. I am married; and therefore my childlessness is shared. My partner has become childless, because of my infertility.

Beginning at the beginning

Each story of infertility is sacred and personal. No narrative will be the same. This will become important to remember in the theological reflection which follows. I first became aware of my own journey with the possibility of impotence and infertility shortly before I entered secondary school. It was at the end of a visit to a consultant urologist; I had been born hypospadias, and therefore needed a number of operations as an infant for reconstruction. After the doctor declared that he would not need to see me again, my mother and I left the consulting room; I, however, went back in and asked whether or not I would 'be normal' like 'other boys'. The nurse smiled while the consultant hesitated. 'What do you mean?' was his response. It seemed like lots of walls crashed down, before I eventually said, 'Will I ever be able to . . . you know?' The consultant said he did not know. As I write it is interesting that I remember that the female nurse kept eye contact with my ten-year-old self, while the male doctor looked at my notes. In many ways this conversation was the beginning of a nightmare that sometimes is kept at bay, yet even now still intrudes, grips and shapes the darkness.

While what was said to me was accurate, there was no way of knowing what would happen; there were two longer-term ideas within this conversation that have shaped my own particular journey. The first is that men are hesitant to talk about infertility and childlessness, and the second that fertility and potency are normal for the male psyche. No one had told me that male infertility would be abnormal; I just knew it at a deep level.

This is relatively unsurprising. McCloughry comments, 'Men cannot stray far in a patriarchal society from the fact that it is the erect penis that symbolizes masculinity.'[143] There is little wonder then that men who cannot father children, or maintain erections, feel themselves not to be as male as those who can. The penis has been seen as the source of life and power. Therefore, if it does not function properly, or is perceived not to, then psychological problems can occur. Both women and men do suffer 'anxiety, stress and depression' after a diagnosis of infertility,[144] but for a man infertility and impotence can seemingly strip him of his masculinity; as much as I imagine a woman who cannot bear life will be plunged into unimaginable agony. The story of the infertile male is, though, less frequently told, cloaked as it too often is with invisibility.

At school, between the ages of twelve and fourteen, one of the nightmares of the week for me was the necessary shower after Physical Education. In common with most boys born with hypospadias, it took a year or so longer than normal for my genitalia to develop 'adequately'. They were a painful two years. Children, as we know, are not the most tactful of human beings, and I can recall with relative ease comments and jocular barbs made. I would, as a result, create a wonderful tapestry

143 Roy McCloughry, *Men and Masculinity*, Hodder & Stoughton, 1992, p. 174.

144 A. Bagshawe and A. Taylor, 'ABC of Subfertility: Couselling', *British Medical Journal*, 1 November 2003, Vol. 327, p. 1038.

of stories for reasons that I did not need to engage with PE and more particularly not have to endure the hell of 'shower time'.

No one had yet introduced me to notions that each human is made in the image of God, expressed both by the Psalmist and by St Irenaeus with his theological dictum, 'The glory of God is a human being fully alive.' Nor had I grappled with Rowan Williams's observation that most human beings have the profound ability to create – and believe – the illusion that they are supremely 'potent'.[145] More importantly, notions of God being in some sense impotent were far from me. For most of us God is all-powerful. Christians familiar with liturgical tradition are shaped by creedal statements that make God an all-powerful imperial figure. Within popular Christian thought, God is all too often a strutting deity rather than, as Nancy Eiesland articulated in the figure of Jesus of Nazareth, 'the disabled God'.[146] Indeed, there have been times in my dance with childlessness that I have sought succour in the thought that God is always wholly Other; and both potent and fertile. This is something I have needed, as I have collided again and again with the 'brick wall of faith' and the sometimes eerie silence of the scriptures concerning the *Sitz im Leben* of those not blessed with children.

This silence compounds the negativity of the words we use to describe those who cannot have children: barren or infertile as opposed to fertile, child*less* as opposed to parent or those with children; sterile as opposed to fruitful. It is a web of prose that can create despair rather than hope. Elaine Tyler May writes, '"Barren" is a term laden with historical weight. It carries negative meanings: unproductive, sterile, bare, empty, stark, deficient, lacking, wanting, destitute, devoid. It is the opposite of fertile, lavish, abounding, productive.'[147]

145 Rowan Williams, *On Christian Theology*, Blackwell, 1999, p. 173.

146 N. L. Eiesland, *The Disabled God: Towards a Liberatory Theology of Disability*, Abingdon Press, 1994, pp. 98–100.

147 E. Tyler May, *Barren in the Promised Land*, Harvard University Press, 1995, p. 11.

The web of negativity is not, though, woven by words alone, but rather by totality of the infertile condition. This includes the fact that the ability to reproduce is taken for granted, regardless of the statistics; as well as the mood music created by expectant grandparents, aunts, uncles and godparents. There will be few parents who do not dream of being grandparents. Friends also can collude in creating a culture of expectation. For just as singles can struggle to fit in a world created for or by couples, couples without children can find it difficult in a world that is seemingly shaped in the image of a parent. While I am grateful for all those who have stood alongside me in the dance; there have been others who have not been able to. This has often been my fault; 'Our words', suggests Rowan Williams, 'strengthen the illusions with which we surround, protect and comfort ourselves.'[148]

Having children can be one of the most human things to do. If a woman cannot bear a child or a man cannot produce effective sperm, there is usually a feeling of inadequacy. In my own case the words 'firing blanks' written in my medical notes was both an illuminating (is that how I am to be seen) and a dehumanizing experience. The feminist theologian, Mary Daly, coined a now famous dictum: 'If God is male; male is God.' Using the same inimitable logic, then also: 'If God is potent; the potent is God.'[149]

The infertile condition is perhaps made worse by the fact that diagnosis is not always clear-cut. Mary Warnock writes, 'The psychological distress [of not being able to conceive] is particularly hard to bear because, except in a minority of cases, a couple cannot know they are not going to conceive. They may continue to hope, as the months go by, and be endlessly disappointed.'[150] For me there has often been the agony of hopefulness. The embrace

148 Rowan Williams, *Silence and Honey Cakes*, Lion, 2003.

149 Mary Daly, *Beyond God the Father: Towards a Philosophy of Women's Liberation*, Women's Press, 1986, p. 9.

150 M. Warnock, *Making Babies: Is there a Right to have Children?*, Oxford University Press, 2002, p. 40.

of this desperate kind of hope is an integral part of the dance. In terms of the Christian tradition I have found it necessary to engage with the scriptures and begin to re-imagine God.

Colliding with the scriptures

Within the biblical text, those who seem to be infertile are invariably granted children, beginning with Genesis, with the stories of Abram and Sarai, Rebecca and Isaac, and Jacob and Rachel. Sarai gives birth to Isaac, Rebecca to Esau and Jacob, and Rachel to Joseph and Benjamin. On the one hand, Isaac, Jacob and Joseph are key figures in the story of the divine relationship with the people of God, and the fact that their births were miraculous or unexpected heightens their importance.

On the other hand, a number of emotions are captured extremely well within these key stories. Some of the pain of childlessness is captured in Abram's lament to his God, which is uttered in response to the divine promise of greatness (Genesis 15.1).

> Abram replied, 'Lord God, what can you give me, seeing that I am childless? The heir to my household is Eliezer of Damascus. You have given me no children, and so my heir must be a slave born in my house.' (Genesis 15.2 REB)

Abram's lament finds added poignancy in the later cry from the heart of Rachel to be given children or to be allowed to die (Genesis 30.1). Some of the jealousy that some of us who are childless from time to time feel against those who have children is captured too. It is evident in Sarai's outburst against Hagar, her slave girl and mother to Abram's first born (Genesis 16.5–6). Rachel is jealous of her sister Leah who can bear Jacob children (Genesis 30.2). Moreover, it is Isaac who is depicted as interceding on behalf of his wife Rebecca. This may be to portray the patriarch in a positive light, but it reflects the actual situation of many infertile couples. It is often the one who is presumed to be fertile who has the emotional energy to pray and/or seek advice. Despite this capturing of emotion, the narrator does not deal with childlessness in a positive way. It is done so coldly. Nowhere is it as clinical as the interchange between Abram and Sarai about Hagar.

> Sarai complained to Abram, 'I am being wronged; you must do something about it. It was I who gave my slave-girl into your arms, but since she has known that she is pregnant, she has despised me. May the Lord see justice done between you and me.' Abram replied,'Your slave-girl is in your hands; deal with her as you please.' (Genesis 16.5–6 REB)

Anyone who has danced with childlessness will feel some empathy with Sarai's plight, except perhaps the Abram depicted by the narrator. There is no hint of feeling for the one who has borne a son or for the one who feels it is impossible for her to do so.[151] Childlessness seems to be solely recorded in the Genesis narrative in order to demonstrate God's own potency to bring life out of barren situations. Perhaps it is not going too far to say that infertility is used as a pawn to add pathos to the significance of the children born.

The New Testament Gospels all begin their introduction to the public ministry of Jesus with reference to the preaching of John the Baptist. Luke alone, however, gives details of his birth. Like Samuel and Samson, the Baptist's parents Zechariah and Elizabeth were unable to have children. Like Abram and Sarai, they would seem now to be too old (Luke 1.7). Unlike Rachel and Hannah, there is no recorded prayer offered, although given Zechariah's social standing as a priest, their childlessness would not have gone unnoticed, hence Elizabeth's comment, 'This is the Lord's doing; now at last he has shown me favour and taken away from me the disgrace of childlessness' (Luke 1.25 REB).

As with the Old Testament passages, the child born (John, who became the Baptist) has a key role to play in the

151 T. Dennis, *Looking God in the Eye*, SPCK, 1998, pp. 50–1.

salvation story; thus his own part in the narrative is given additional impetus by the unusual naturalness surrounding his conception.

Childlessness seems to be used throughout the biblical tradition as a literary device pointing to the importance of the one born. As such, childlessness is not addressed as an issue per se. However, the biblical narrators never see childlessness as something positive; rather it is always something to be taken away. The biblical text alludes to some of the emotions that can surround infertility: shame, rivalry and jealousy.

It is the fact that childlessness is used in this way that is acutely problematic. While it does add drama to the story; it is always a sub-plot, and within the sub-plot the director's notes are negative; even if the negativity is not explicitly stated. So for example, Sarai's shame is removed: for she is able to provide a son for Abram. Similarly, the disgrace of Elizabeth is removed by her conception. There is nothing, therefore, for those of us who dance with childlessness to take from these sacred stories except the conundrum that God is able to intervene. This is precisely because no childless couple remains without children in the divine drama. This is something that cannot and should not be ignored.

Furthermore, within the canon, the couples who are given children are not allowed to keep them. Hannah hands over Samuel to the Temple. This was part of her promise to God if she was granted a son. Isaac, the longed-promised one is saved from being a sacrificial offering by the horns of a ram and the thorns of a bush. Isaac is part of the divine plan – and seems to belong to God rather than to Abraham and Sarah.

Samson and the Baptist are both 'holy men'. They are given over to the service to God. This is particularly telling of John the Baptist. He was born to a priest and therefore would have been expected to fulfil the functions of the priestly caste of his day. Are we to believe that Zechariah and Elizabeth would not have been a little disappointed that their son seemed to sacrifice his career prospects in exchange for a diet of locusts and honey?

The pattern of God giving and taking away children is uniquely seen in the life of Jesus. The child given to Mary of Nazareth does not fully belong to her. He never seems to be wholly hers in the time between the two cradlings. That of the suckling new born and of the broken and battered body, removed from a Roman gallows.

I have had the good fortune to have worked in the field of biblical studies; and therefore am aware that our sacred texts come from a particular cultural milieu, and that through attentively listening to the textual settings the overall message can be hopeful rather than oppressive. However, as a priest, familiar with the liturgical rhythm of the daily Offices, I am acutely aware of the divine pronouncements that declare that children are a blessing, and contrariwise the lack of children should be taken as a curse. This can make the Bible a harsh book for those who cannot have children. For a while I thought I could take refuge in theologies of liberation. However, there are a number of reasons why such an approach did not take.

First it is arguable that those of us who are childless are not oppressed in the sense that those who are poor in the contexts of liberation are. Those of us who are childless undoubtedly suffer, but we do not necessarily always assume that to have children is a fundamental human right. Many of us, though, will have echoed Rachel's cry. I have – and sometimes still do.

Second, liberation theology almost inevitably involves setting free those who are oppressed and punishing in some form those who are the oppressors. God frees the people of Israel but destroys the armies of Egypt. The danger therefore is that in achieving our own freedom, someone else is oppressed. Childlessness causes pain, but it is hard to know whether there is a 'who' that creates this. There is no obvious Egyptian army at which to vent the divine wrath.

For me then I have had to accept and experience that the scriptures, which I love dearly, collide with my childlessness. They have the effect of jolting me in the dance with childlessness. In a sense, collision is true of all interpretive acts with a text.[152] There is a tension between experiences, cultures and imaginations of the writer and reader. This is magnified by the distance of time when applied to the scriptures. Personally, it is an exhausting and fruitless exercise to attempt a rescue mission on various stories and pericopaes within the sacred text. Instead, I have sought solace in what the God of the Bible might be like.

Encountering an impotent God

One of my most vivid memories of Secondary School are the wet days that meant that Physical Education could not be done outside. With only one dedicated gymnasium, this meant that boys and girls would be put together. In my school this meant only one thing: barn dances. Mr Hill and Mrs Cadona put on some country and western musak and we were away. We sniggered through the Gay Gordons and the Dashing White Sergeant. At certain times in a dance, each one of us would try to invert the order so that we did not dance with those we did not want to. Sometimes this inevitably meant that on occasion, when Mrs Cadona – and it was always she – yelled, 'Change partner', we found ourselves looking at the face of someone who we did not expect. This is how it was the first time I began to think of an impotent God; my breath was for a moment taken away.

There are others who are already on the journey of re-imagining what the biblical God might be like, for example, Eiesland writes, 'For me, epiphanies come too infrequently to be shrugged off as unbelievable. Like a faithful Jew who had conscientiously opened the door for Elijah each Seder . . . I had waited for a mighty revelation of God. But my epiphany bore lit-

152 The idea of collision being an interpretative act was introduced to me by Bishop Gordon Mursell who came to lead a community meeting when I was ordained at the Queen's Foundation in Birmingham. Bishop Gordon was then Dean of Birmingham.

tle resemblance to the God I was expecting . . . I saw God in a sip-puff wheelchair.'[153]

For Eiesland this vision of God reveals one who is incarnate for her. This may inevitably lead to concern that God is being made in the image of Eiesland. There are perhaps two ways to counter such thought. The first would be to remind ourselves that God is so often depicted in our own image. The second way is the reminder that the Christian faith has a disabled God at its very core: the human Jesus on the cross; disability is not only present on the cross, but afterwards in the risen Jesus.

Luke tells of the post-Easter walk of two disciples from Jerusalem to Emmaus when, unknown to them, they are accompanied by Jesus. While Jesus is able to explain to them 'the whole of scripture', they only recognize him as their rabbi when his scarred hands break the bread (Luke 24.25–32). 'In presenting his impaired hands and feet to his startled friends, the resurrected Jesus is revealed as the disabled God.'[154] The Revelation to St John holds on to a similar tradition. In the heavenly court, the one deemed worthy to open the secrets of the universe is none other than a wounded lamb (Revelation 5.6), and the praise offered to this unlikeliest of creatures echoes this theme (Revelation 5.9).

McCloughry and Morris, writing in response to Eiesland, make the comment: 'In a suffering world, Christians can hold their heads up. For our God is not a distant God of power who ignores the cries of the oppressed, but a disabled God, a wounded God, whose wounds will never disappear throughout eternity.'[155]

One would have to say that this is not the God that most people of faith envisage, there is a sense that the wounds of Christ are rendered out of focus by the brightness and glory of our resurrection images. Moreover there would be many who

153 Eiesland, *The Disabled God*, p. 89.

154 Eiesland, *The Disabled God*, p. 100.

155 R. Mccloughry and W. Morris, *Making a World of Difference: Christian Reflections on Disability*, SPCK, 2002, p. 69.

would feel cheated by a disabled or wounded deity, and more still alarmed at the possibility of a God who is in some sense powerless or impotent.

This is not how God is supposed to be. I am reminded of the film *The Wizard of Oz*, which chronicles the journey of Dorothy, the Scarecrow, Tin Man and Cowardly Lion to the Emerald City. They are off to see the wonderful Wizard. What they find is an aged man behind a curtain who is not at all powerful, just someone else desperate, like Dorothy, to get home. The travellers are disappointed. One might imagine that Christians would be disappointed at a God who is at times powerless. They would feel cheated, for it is simply not how God is supposed to be. I have found this not to be the case, as I have allowed the fact of Holy Saturday, of the dead corpse of Jesus of Nazareth, to be a particular prism through which to see God.

The problem with the lifeless body of Jesus as an image of God is Easter Day. For while there is little room for doubt that the broken and dead body of Jesus taken from the cross and embalmed by friends before being placed in the tomb of a relative stranger represents the epitome of impotence; it is rightly obscured by the resurrection. Herein lies the point – it is obscured but should not be forgotten. For Alan Lewis – the Jesus of late Good Friday and Holy Saturday is caught between yesterday and tomorrow. For the western Church of the twenty-first century, the glory of the resurrection may always be here, but Lewis reminds us that the first Saturday would have seemed empty. There would have been no looking forward, and reflection on the day before – if that were possible for Jesus' friends – would have been 'intrinsically unbearable'.[156]

David Ford reminds us that, just as the risen Jesus cannot be separated from the one hanging on the cross, the risen Jesus cannot be separated from the corpse lying in the tomb. The dead Christ should, he argues, influence our understanding of who Jesus is. 'His lordship has this death, this tortured, bloody

156 Alan Lewis, *The Theology of Holy Saturday: Between Cross and Resurrection*, W. B. Eerdmans, 2001, p. 43.

and dead face, always at its heart.'[157] If this means that we see the divine in a different light, it means also that we are called to experience life differently, for Ford continues,

> It portrays a way of love whose normal fate, given the way human beings and the world are, is suffering, concealment, misunderstanding, humiliation to the point of martyrdom.

Yet, this looking at God as impotent or powerless is not something we try to do, instead God remains almost automatically powerful, and therefore alienating for a number of people, including some of us who struggle with childlessness. The default position for Christian theologians is of God defined by omnipotence, omniscience and omnipresence. Yet Holy Saturday does speak of a God who is broken and wasted. The broken body of Jesus might speak specifically to those who struggle with pain and want to cling on to God, including those who are childless because the broken body belongs to another 'who has lived for God and for others and has trusted in God even in death'.[158] As I meditate on the possibility that my infertility might be connected in some way with the death of Jesus, I recall a friend's assertion that living with infertility might be described as a form of 'genetic death'. It is not that the death of Christ makes sense of all suffering or that infertility, suddenly for the believer, becomes more palatable when confronted by the dead Christ; rather it serves as a reminder of Paul's assertion that in living as Christians we carry around the death of Christ in some sense.

> But we have this treasure in clay jars, so that it might be clear that this extraordinary power belongs to God and does not come from us. We are afflicted in every way, but not crushed; perplexed but not driven to despair; persecuted, but not forsaken, struck down, but not destroyed; always

157 David Ford, *Self and Salvation*, Cambridge University Press, 1999, p. 204.

158 Ford, *Self and Salvation*, p. 206.

> carrying in the body the death of Jesus, so that the life of Jesus may also be made visible in our bodies. For while we live, we are always being given up to death for Jesus' sake, so that the life of Jesus may be made visible in our mortal flesh. (2 Corinthians 4.7–11)

Some of this passage is immediately alienating, for there have been times in my own quest for children when words like crushed, despairing and forsaken would have seemed quite appropriate. Yet, in this passage the themes of death, mortality and hope are intertwined. The passage is part of Paul's overall defence of his apostolic ministry. Larry Kreitzer writes, 'There were some who interpreted Paul's suffering and physical weakness as a sign of divine displeasure, if not punishment.'[159] Paul, however, turns such an argument on its head; far from it; his weakness, his impotence was part of the suffering and barrenness of God in Christ. While Paul is not referring explicitly to childlessness, there is a good reason for thinking that infertility is implicitly caught up in the phrase 'always carrying in the body the death of Jesus'. The word 'death' is translated from the Greek *nekrosis*, which Paul uses on only one other occasion, Romans 4.19, where he is referring to Sarah's barrenness.[160] Might it be possible therefore for the dead and broken body of Christ to give hope to those who carry death around with them? Such a possibility gives me profound hope that my infertility can be brought in from the shadows. Almost immediately however, I am confronted with the truth that the dead Jesus is usually too quickly transformed into a living Lord, and weaknesses generally airbrushed out by strengths. Rowan Williams aptly sums up the situation: it is 'a bitter paradox' when 'Easter hymns and Easter preaching . . . bury the reality of the crucified'.[161] Sadly the story

159 Larry Kreitzer, *2 Corinthians*, Academic Press, 1996, p. 101.

160 V. P. Furnish, *II Corinthians*, Doubleday, 1985, pp. 255–6.

161 R. Williams, W. H. Vanstone et. al., 'Buried in Truth', in *Darkness Yielding: Angles on Christmas, Holy Week and Easter*, Cairns Publications, 2001, p. 244.

of the powerless God at the heart of the Christian tradition is too quickly removed from the Christian narrative.

However, the model of a corpse as a symbol of salvation cannot give us hope if it is an end in and of itself. Nor can it simply be overlaid by the glories of resurrection. But it does convince me that we have a God who knows what it means to work within the limits of our mortality rather than against them. For me this has been the beginning, not of an answer to my childlessness, but of how it is possible to talk to God about the pain that has shaped our dance. The Christian hope is that when we look into the face of God, we see someone who is 'Other', but also 'Similar'; not for me always 'Potent' but sometimes 'Impotent'. The Christian deity is one whose eyes betray the pain of suffering on the cross, but also the pain, frustration and yearning at being powerless in the face of wanting to do something. Yet, while this is true, the face of God also shows a delight of life,and a glory in living. Childlessness is the pain that has shaped rather than stopped the dance.

I am aware of friends who have found that childlessness, and the web of negativity that surrounds it, stifles their lives. This has not been so for me. It could have been. Indeed, at times, it perhaps has done. Childlessness does this because it robs humans of particular futures. It does invisibly. It is this that is insidious.

As a person of faith, a Christian, a priest, I am aware that easy answers for those who long for children are hollow, unreal and unhelpful responses. The scriptures are to be wrestled with, even endured. The God found in the Bible gives hope, for that God is someone I have found joins me in the myriad of dances contained within the infertile journey. This is again the beginning; one that is filled with pain, for in joining in the dance there is affirmation that it is a dance that does not end. I have discovered, though, that it in the tears and laughter, the joy and pain that there is nothing better than the dance with the impotent God.

10

Snapshots of an Illness

PETER KERR

Only the echoes of my mind.[162]

My illness and my portion

I have lived with leukaemia for sixteen years. I have discovered that it is a 'disease' of the mind as well as the blood and bone marrow. For me, living with chronic illness is as much about neutering the power of mind games as it is about management of physical symptoms.

I am ambivalent about sharing what goes on inside my head. My struggle with mortality is a private one, but by no means unique. It is arguable that chronic illness in one's sixth decade poses similar challenges to the inevitable process of ageing. What follows is a reflection on the normal physical and mental stress of growing old accentuated by the abnormality of a particular terminal condition. The reader will have to forgive me if articulating these 'echoes of my mind' strays into self-indulgence.

My struggle may not be unique but my illness is unique *to me* and so in a sense sacred, an aspect of my vocation as a human being and a priest. To lay it bare sometimes feels like a violation. It has been a central part of my life for the past sixteen years, a constantly changing challenge against which I continue to shape my identity. Public disclosure assumes an intimacy

162 Fred Neil, 1966, 'Everybody's talkin', sung by Harry Nilsson, released by Capitol, 1969. Theme song from *Midnight Cowboy*, United Artists, 1969.

that is often beyond that which I share with many friends and some family and therefore is not to be contemplated lightly. On the other hand, the discipline of writing for publication may be the only way for a person like me properly to appropriate this 'apprenticeship'. So I am first and foremost writing, as I preach, for myself.

There will be six sections in the chapter. It begins with the story of my illness over the past sixteen years. There follow four sections which interpret my illness from different perspectives. I will call them 'truths': Body Truth, Private Truth, Public Truth and Present Truth. Together they explore from a variety of angles the tension between suffering a private illness and living it publicly – 'soul pain'. Finally there is a short postscript.

It all started when I was fifty and beginning to think about changing jobs. I had the first hints of illness in the local Methodist Church Hall which, in weekdays, doubles up as the Blood Donation Centre (it's still difficult to go past it without just a fleeting intimation of doom). I had given blood before and I knew the drill. To my surprise, I was told to make an appointment with my GP as my blood wasn't quite right. 'Probably the after effects of a cold' they said, which seemed likely as I had had an obstinate cough since the previous Easter. But I thought no more of it and booked a blood test. A week or so later my GP broke the bad news. Things moved fast. An appointment was made with a consultant haematologist. It was a bright summer's morning when Diane and I drove to the hospital out-patients' ward which, for the next seven or so years, until its closure, came to be a powerful symbol of my real or imagined tenuous hold on life. I was met by a brusque but homely nurse who bluntly told me that the only thing to do was to accept my fate and get used to it. At the time her advice was as comforting as an ice-cold shower on a winter's day but, on reflection, sensible and honest. I was released back into the morning sun about an hour later with a prescription for some red pills. The feeling of relief on release from the hospital has never lessened in intensity despite, at time of writing, having to attend every three to four weeks. I diffused the shock by talking at Diane all the way home: 'Would I be around for my daughter's wedding and/or should I record my speech now and "appear" as the disembodied father of the bride?' She listened.

My leukaemia is Chronic Lymphocytic Leukaemia or CLL. Like all cancers it is a non-invasive organism and so part of my makeup. It is the price I pay for being me.[163] This is comforting because it means a particular treatment may work with my body even though it has failed on others. My basic problem, according to a cheerful young registrar, is that I 'can't hold my blood'. It may be a disease of the blood, but for me it is a disease of the bones, the bone marrow to be precise. One of the most feared of the routine medical procedures is the bone marrow test which uses the crudest of tools to bore into what seems like the very heart of my being. Maybe that is why the weekly orange pill I take to strengthen my bones seems so ominous.

> My life is consumed with anguish and my years with groaning.
> My strength fails because of my affliction.
> And my bones grow weak. (Psalm 31.10 NIV)

Fifty is a young age to develop CLL. By all accounts I am doing well to have survived so long, 'well beyond your shelf-life' according to a cheery male nurse. Management of the disease ranges from daily pill popping, through chemotherapy to frequent blood transfusions and monoclonal antibody treatments. I am prey to dangerous infections which have required surgery. My medical routine is a day visit to hospital for a monthly infusion of whatever drug has been most recently prescribed, along with a quarterly visit to my consultant. That is safe normality for me.

I cope with appointments by my mind game of 'at least'. Let me explain. I can remember emerging into the morning sunshine with a sigh of relief after an early appointment and saying to myself, 'Well at least they haven't put me on the ward . . . or started me on one of those awful treatments that others further down the line casually mentioned.' Gradually, the 'at leasts'

163 'Defeating Cancer', *Horizon*, BBC 2, 10.4.2012.

got more desperate as the disease progressed. After the first embarrassing experience of being cannulated by a junior doctor who managed to spray my blood all over the floor, I thought 'at least they didn't put me to bed' and after a more intense bout of treatment; 'at least they didn't do a bone marrow test'.

Changes in treatment routines are always difficult, most memorably, when rumours began to circulate about the building of a new hospital. We long-term patients were given little official notice of the new 'home' in which we were destined to spend a lot of time for the remainder of our lives. It looked like a high security prison from the outside, but on entry had the feel of a spacious airport concourse which to this day strangely lifts my spirits, perhaps because it suggests holiday time. The change-over to the new premises took place over just one weekend. The suddenness seemed shocking. Most of us patients inevitably preferred the old one. Living with terminal illness, we instinctively seemed to know that the priority for us was familiar care in a familiar place rather than computerized procedures in a state-of-the-art environment. Turnover in staff, increasingly frequent, has also been difficult. Close and healing relationships are inevitably built up over the years. P . . ., if it fitted his schedule, would give me a lift to the hospital. P . . . and A . . . despite being rushed off their feet took the time to build a friendship. Later when I was suddenly moved downstairs it felt like a mix of being jilted and bereaved.

The most difficult change was the retirement of my consultant after a fourteen-year relationship. He accompanied me in a journey which has gone from the possibility of fairly imminent death to the miracle of remission, always with honest, respectful care and a steely determination. He was a 'proper' doctor dressed immaculately in white coat, collar and tie and well-polished shoes. He always respected the doctor–patient relationship, addressing me in his soft Scots accent as 'Mr Kerr'. He preferred homely euphemisms when describing the more scary treatments. 'Putting a bit more spirit in your preaching' was the code for a blood transfusion, and blood counts if mentioned were just either 'a wee bit low', or 'good enough'. 'Empowering the patient' may not have been a phrase that tripped off his lips, but he brought reassurance to one who often felt that he sat in 'darkness and the shadow of death'.[164] I wrote about him in the parish magazine.[165]

Notes from the Blue Chair

The reclining chairs in Laurel 3 Day Patients, where I am spending much of my time at the moment, are an aquamarine Mediterranean blue. A pillow with a fresh white pillow case awaits me each morning. You can have your favourite seat and even a cup of coffee if you arrive early enough.

A few weeks ago I noticed an invitation to a retirement party for my consultant pinned on the opposite wall to my favourite chair. Everything in me said NO! When for so long you've had those sensitive fingers exploring glands in places you didn't even know you had them, you don't let go without a struggle. But let go I must.

The cure rate for leukaemia is not at the top of the league for cancers. But even if there can be no cure, there can always be healing. Healing happens when the patient feels listened to and known, is treated like an individual, and feels part of a trusted relationship of healing. This requires the doctor to risk the cost of offering such a relationship.

This is the ministry, and mystery of redemption, the work of bringing good from evil, of helping people to put together the broken pieces of their lives. It is supremely what God does and it is the task with which he asks us to collaborate. Dr A . . . collaborated at some cost. He offered an honest hope of redemption, a must for those who would live with cancer. By what he was, as much as what he did, he has helped those of us reclining in the blue chairs to put ourselves back together again.

164 Benedictus, *Book of Common Prayer*.
165 Ombersley and Doverdale, Parish Magazine, February 2012.

On 7 September 2007. I had noted:

> Dr A . . . at the 20th anniversary celebration of my induction to the parish last night. To my surprise, there he was, standing shyly on the edge of things.

That was as powerful an act of healing as any he had prescribed down the years.

Other patients often had just as an important role to play in healing. I remember being given an hour's notice to pack my things and get up to hospital on threat of forfeiting my hard won bed. I arrived in the ward in which there were already three other patients. It felt strange and alien. It always does, no matter how many times you've been before. I felt totally disconnected. However, we patients had one thing in common: the bodily functions or, more accurately, dysfunctions. So the ice was soon broken, conversations began. The strangers were becoming people. We were connecting, discovering a fellowship even if it was the fellowship of the damned. In trusting ourselves to each other we were creating a healing community energized by that 'anonymous third person who makes the introductions, acts as go-between, makes two beings aware of each other, sets up a current of communication between them' and whose name for Christians is the Holy Spirit or 'Go-between God'.[166]

This current of communication is perhaps more akin to that of the battlefield,[167] for my chronic cancer isn't so much a lone struggle against the illness but more a battle where your fellow combatants are, sometimes, just as important to the outcome as those (doctors and nurses) directing the battle. And

166 John Taylor, *The Go-between God*, SCM Press, 1972, p. 17.

167 Danny Baker, 'You don't fight cancer, you are the battlefield, Normandy Beach, Hastings 1066', 'You, Me and The Big C', *Guardian Weekend*, 10/03/12.

some don't make it. Sometimes on asking after the progress of a particular patient you would simply be met with a sad smile and shrug . . . and you knew. There was Z . . ., a tapestry restorer in her early twenties, and Sister Margaret Mary, a nun from Stanbrooke Abbey, their deaths unacknowledged publicly in the ward. And what of young W. . .? Only silence. The Psalmist's reassurance is welcome, while also eliciting inevitable survivor's guilt:

> You will not fear . . .
> the pestilence that stalks in darkness
> or the destruction that wastes at noonday.
> A thousand may fall at your side,
> Ten thousand at your right hand (Psalm 91.5–7)

And that is 'my portion'.

Body truth

> You have knitted me together in my mother's womb. (Psalm 139.13)

On 7 February 2010, I jotted down:

> Long treatment day . . . barren zombie! Feel nothing; . . . empty. Light a candle. Walk to Church, kneel by my Jacobean altar. Do something physical. Get the body working. After all that's what has got me into this mess.

That's what I call body truth. Truth is embodied, The Word is enfleshed. So he who 'knitted me together in my mother's womb' (Psalm 139.13) is known to me through my body, blood, bones and cancer. If my body is sick, I am sick, for I *am* my body[168] and my healing – or wholeness – is the spiritual and physical strength to be human in sickness and in health. It is no surprise that Jesus, who came that we might have abundant life, was popularly known as a healer and as one who knew that our destiny and identity are bound up with our bodies.

So what about my body? I am male, over six feet tall and about fourteen stone in weight. My body is sixty-five years old with the usual attendant characteristics of late middle age; a bit of arthritis in my fingers, baldness (since my twenties), a back that needs watching and one tooth short of a set. I have a surgically related hernia which embarrassingly gives me a pregnant bump. According to my mother my best features were my long legs ('should have been a girl' – wasn't!) and my long tapering fingers ('should have become a pianist' – didn't!). For much of the time I feel well.

But my body is also sick. It has been officially sick for sixteen years now and I have several huge medical files to prove it. At first there were few physical symptoms. Later, more worrying signs began to appear: spontaneous bruising, bleeding from the gums – usually nocturnal – and, later still, a low blood count which meant increasingly regular blood transfusions. On 20 December 2001, six years after diagnosis, I noted that I was 'living on lots of borrowed blood'. I suffered pneumococal infections in both my hip and knee which required surgery and then, most recently, the splendectomy. I never really acknowledged that I had cancer until I lost my spleen. Somehow the violation of my abdomen was the wake-up call. It was only after ten years that I finally heard my body tell me that I was seriously ill despite, for most of the time, barring stays in hospital, being able to lead a normal life.

In hospital, my body and its needs took over. It rarely allowed me to forget for very long that I was sick. I described one visit.

---

168 Elisabeth Moltmann-Wendel *I am My Body*, SCM Press, 1994, pp. 22–3.

It is very early; maybe about 0300 hrs on a December morning in my 59th year. I wake after a few hours restless sleep. My body is in revolt against the removal of my spleen a fortnight earlier. It registers its protest not only in the discomfort of my violated abdomen, but in the huge swollen and very painful lymph nodes on the right side of my neck. 'Bad news for a leukaemia sufferer,' I think. But my mind is in catch-up mode. My body is in charge now, reasserting itself, refusing to be the anonymous tool for existence any longer. At that moment my body was me, 100%. And I was miserable. Waves of self-pity threatened to overwhelm:

Can I move my legs?
How can I stop this pain?
Can I have a urine jug and quickly?
I can't cope with all these tubes,
Please do something with these damned pillows,
I wish my bowels would move.
Will I ever get to sleep with the lights on?
I don't want another infusion . . . and not with that bully of a nurse.
Why doesn't the toast come before the tea is cold?

Surprisingly, everything that I thought might be a comfort and strength – reading the Psalms, praying, even Holy Communion – seemed emotionally neutral. *Take it or leave it was* my attitude. Other people, other bodies were what were important; they were the people who took care of my body and who by their sensitivity recognized it was *my* body and not just any body, not easy when a catheter is being inserted. I remember wishing that someone would bathe my feet in warm water and rub them with a towel, a *'prayer'* that was answered nearly immediately and, to me, miraculously, by a busy nurse who was later embarrassed to be addressed by me as 'angel'. The angels ministered to me, as to Jesus in the desert.

Beyond the hospital it was healing to know that so many others were praying for me and my body. I felt I was being carried, a bit like the paralysed man who was let down through the roof where Jesus was teaching so that he might be healed. His healing was a gift from others who trusted.

I have always resented being defined by my sick body. I am not just the Vicar who has leukaemia. But then my insistent body reminds me yet again that I am my body, my sick body. Those sharp reminders come very obviously through tiredness, swellings or pain; sometimes, more confusingly, when I am ambushed by inexplicable invective and black depression. Then with the Psalmist I protest God's idiocy and strategic naivety:

> Shall your love be declared in the grave:
> or your faithfulness in the place of destruction?
> Will your wonders be made known in the dark:
> or your righteousness in the land where all things are forgotten? (Psalm 88.12–13 AS)

Many times just before an appointment I fall. I cannot help myself going down into the slough of despond or being irrationally short with those closest to me. It is as if something is stirring up the black slime at the bottom of the pond of my consciousness which envelops me to the extent that I become powerless to be civil. I prefer at these times to be alone and to travel alone to hospital. But the slime settles on the bottom again and I regain perspective and surprise myself with a new zest for life. It is a constant stomach-churning roller-coaster of a ride, an experience memorably captured in Thomas Merton's poem 'All the Way Down'. Everyone thought he had gone for ever 'all the way in hell', but he 'got right back into my body and came out/And rang my bell'.[169] I love that bell!

We speak quite casually of coming 'down' with something or 'falling' ill without giving much thought to the significance of what we are saying. To fall is to be surprised; to be out of control, falling down 'lower than Jonas', as Merton describes.

169 Thomas Merton, *All the Way Down*, cited by Paul Murray in *The Spirituality of Bewilderment*, Columba Press, 2002.

There is not just one falling. It is repeated over a long period of illness but it always surprises with the intensity of its black despair. Targets are inched towards, the day for the operation, news of the scan, the progress report on treatment, the release date from hospital. Then, in a moment, sometimes rather casually, the bad news is broken and the target, so carefully anticipated over weeks or months, assumes total irrelevance. It's back to square one, another falling ill as unprepared for as the first.

> It is rather like an endless game of Snakes and Ladders. I am doing well . . . when the dice suddenly lands me on the wrong square and I find myself back down the snake again.[170]

As with any extreme physical challenge, critical illness brings an intensity of feeling to living. *Now* is the time, the only time. The present moment consumes any concern about the future. Its intensity fills the most routine of duties. I was giving my granddaughter her final bottle just before bed. Holding and feeding our own granddaughter was something I thought I might not get an opportunity to do a few years ago when I was seriously ill. I fed her nourishment and as she sucked and rested quietly in my arms (nearly asleep) she filled my being with contentment and thanks. I held Natasha and through her God held both of us within the everlasting circle of his love, a circle which included my mother who had held me in the same way. The circle was complete. 'I have calmed and quieted my soul, like a weaned child with its mother' (Psalm 131.2).

In contrast was the intensity of 'wild water' as a cleansing agent. I remember in the early stages of illness, on the completion of a course of chemotherapy treatment, I went with my brother to the North Antrim Coast in Ulster to spend a few days visiting our old boyhood haunts. It was in May, I think, and we drove to a favourite rock pool on the spectacular Atlantic coast.

170 Barbara Baisley, *No Easy Answers*, Epworth, 2000, p. 11.

Despite the inevitable shock of the water temperature at that time of year I plunged in to the clear blue sea with a shout of liberation: 'cleansed, cleansed from those b . . . chemicals!' I was right back into my body and ringing my bell.

In periods of remission, strange though it may seem, I miss that intensity of experience. It is recaptured sometimes in the quality of silence before a candle in church and the feeling of quiet reassurance as the smoke from the snuffed candle releases my often inarticulate groans and wafts them upwards, rough, raw material for Christ's ministry of constant intercession to the Father.

Out of hospital and between routine appointments my body is less insistent and I quickly relapse into comfortable mind–body dualism again. I, or my body, forgets the 'snakes' until sharply reminded of them by my weekly loading of the pill box jerking me back into 'body reality', two blue tablets one red twice daily after food. Body Truth is always a life measured out by those pills on the leukaemia snakes and ladders board.

Private truth

The Long Apprenticeship of Assent.[171]

On 1 July 1995, on probable CLL diagnosis, I noted: 'The Lord will fulfil his purpose for me, your steadfast love, O Lord, endures for ever; Do not forsake the work of your hands' (Psalm 138.8).

His purpose is my portion, a vocation I had not envisaged when I was ordained in the early seventies in Belfast. It may seem strange but if you count the hours and days given over to hospitals and appointments and the mental energy expended in thinking, talking, weeping and multiply it all by sixteen years (and whatever is left) then there is no other conclusion than that . . . My job – 'apprenticeship' – is cancer. It's what I do

171 Michael O'Siadhail, 'Threshold', *Our Double Time*, Bloodaxe, 1998.

with my time. It is not something I talk about much. It is the 'private truth' of my living with chronic illness.

During a period of intensive treatment I give my life over to my 'trade'. I get up in the morning, take my pills, pack a lunch. A car calls for me and it's off to the day patients' centre at the local hospital. There I meet and greet my colleagues and fellow workers – nurses and fellow-sufferers – find my 'work station' and begin work. I wait. Some days I wait to get a seat. I wait my turn with the nurses. I wait for the results of a blood test; I wait for treatment to begin, if the tests are OK. Then, when the treatment is done, I wait in case of any adverse effects. I ring my lift and wait to go home. I wait anything from two to six hours, three days a week, sometimes more. I am a patient and *practise* patience. My skill is in learning to be graciously patient. It's my job.

> 'It is the bread that the Lord has given [me] to eat.' (Exodus 16.15)

This vocation is uniquely mine. 'What I do is me: for that I came.'[172]

I used to think it was a sort of extra, a negative add on, which at best I should 'bravely struggle against' or at worst, to which I must resign myself. Now, rather than choose heroic resistance too long a sacrifice makes a stone of the heart,[173] I realize I have got to see it as my work and work has its highs and lows, its Monday and Friday feelings, its victories and defeats, just like my job. We moan at the bosses – the managers and sometimes the consultants and we sympathize with the workers – other patients and nurses. We listen and mutually support.

The problem is that this 'vocation' is only an echo in *my* mind. Others have different ideas for me. They see my

---

172 G. M. Hopkins, 'As Kingfishers Catch Fire', *Selected Poems of Gerard Manley Hopkins*, Heinemann Educational Books, 1961, p. 52.

173 W. B. Yeats, 'Easter 1916', *W. B. Yeats Selected Poetry*, Norman Jeffares, ed., Macmillan/Papermac 1962, p. 93.

'vocation' as a campaign, a struggle to be bravely entered into, and they stand on the side lines and cheer me on rejoicing in the small victories which, I know only too well, are just part of the long war of attrition. Others project unto me extremities of illness and treatment which I know I haven't suffered. ('Well of course you have been there, you know about this better that I do.') I am included in their particular 'cancer gang' as if I was a sort of holy talisman who, if they stay close ('touch the hem of his garment . . .', Matthew 14.36) will lead them through. Is this part of my vocation as a publicly ill parson or am I a fraud? 'Are you better now?' they inquire kindly, in all innocence. 'Of course I'm not,' I want to say, 'this is a life sentence.' 'This is my vocation. It can't be dismissed as comfortably as that!'

I struggle with this and sometimes feel very lonely. My illness is not only my portion but at times a place, a lonely place. American novelist Flannery O'Connor's description of her chronic illness resonates.

> I have never been anywhere but sick. In a sense sickness is a place, more instructive than a long trip to Europe, and it's always a place where there's no company, where nobody can follow.[174]

During remissions as I approach my monthly top-up treatment, the loneliness returns right on time. During the previous twenty-four hours I discover yet again that this is a journey that has to be travelled alone. I shun company. I like to be quiet and on my own as I go through my preparatory ritual; pack a lunch, select some books to fill the six to eight hours, have some breakfast and walk the dog, I look in on the church, always making a point of lighting my prayer candle, a physical gesture which often is my only prayer. I collect the newspaper for the crossword and set off. The dark damp winter mornings are bad. For routine treatment, I like to drive myself as I don't want to talk.

174 Robert Ellsberg, *The Saints' Guide to Happiness*, Darton, Longman and Todd, 2004, p. 119.

The car knows its way. I leave the car at the park-and-ride by the local rugby ground where memories of convivial afternoons always offer a transitory anaesthetic. I join the hospital bus, stare out the window and switch off. Limbo. The bell rings and the driver's brief nod to each of us as we step down, is a final affirmation of freedom. The hardest yards are the short walk up the hill to the hospital. I always go 'lower than Jonas and the whale'. Pure willpower pushes me up that hill. I enter the concourse of the hospital, the factory floor and the start of my 'working day'.

We were warned that the vocation to priesthood would be lonely. But accepting this lonely illness as vocation is hard. I scribbled the question on 28 March 2000, 'In God's pending tray?' It bothered me for some years as I applied, unsuccessfully for other jobs. Glimpses of vocational direction were scarce. But John Henry Newman has always strengthened the frayed cord of purpose:

> God has created me to do Him some definite service . . . Therefore I will trust Him. Whatever, wherever I am, I can never be thrown away. If I am in sickness, my sickness may serve Him; in perplexity, my perplexity may serve Him; if I am in sorrow, my sorrow may serve Him . . . I am a link in a chain, a bond of connection between peoples.[175]

That's it! At least it is a 'definite' enough 'service' for me at the moment. That is what I do during those long days of treatment. I connect,[176] whether it be through sharing a crossword, enquiring of a nurse about her sick partner or responding to queries about what you might call the more technical side of my 'trade' – baptisms, weddings, and times of Christmas services. I sense that there is even an unarticulated perception of

---

175 J. H. Newman, *Meditations and Devotions III*, Longmans Green, 1893, p. 400.

176 Robin Green, *Only Connect*, Darton, Longman and Todd, 1987; a fine reflection on priestly vocation.

me as a sort of go-between between here and 'there', the now and the hereafter.

If this is what I am here for where would I be without my 'job' and what would I do if I was cured? It sort of happened, at the final throw of the dice when other treatments had failed. 'Let's try you on campath,' my consultant announced one day. It is the brand name for a monoclonal antibody treatment which works by boosting one's own natural defences. It worked. 'I came right out and rang my bell!'[177] Blood transfusions no longer required. It was as close to a New Testament healing miracle as I have been. It was a dramatic remission rather than a complete cure and in a funny way more than I had bargained for. It was a bit too close for comfort, a bit too generous. Perceiving God as so directly involved in my healing is disconcerting. I would rather just be in remission. Remission is sometimes easier to deal with than cure. It bears no vocational responsibilities and the unmerited grace of God can be frightening. By nature I probably would have been among the nine lepers who didn't come back to give thanks, I fear.

For sixteen years my private truth is constantly skewed and poisoned by my imagination. It is the killer that threatens the soul. In my imagination I have said my last goodbyes, died and organized fantastic funerals many times. The imagination attracts my worst fears as sure as fruit flies to overripe tomatoes or manure to dung flies. I call it imagination contamination. Insomnia during the lonely watches of the night does not help. Experience, of course, tells me that my anxious imaginations can be put aside for the moment by a dawn walk with the dog, a psalm or the gift of an on-target prayer. Particularly effective in this respect has been:

> Do not look forward to what might happen tomorrow,
> The same everlasting Father who cares for you today
> Will take care of you tomorrow and every day . . .

177 Merton, *All the Way Down.*

> Be at peace then and put aside all anxious thoughts and imaginations.
> Do not look forward to what might happen tomorrow and put aside all anxious thoughts and imaginations.[178]

And what if I were to be totally cured? Of course it would be wonderful. Yet I risk losing that urgency and intensity which can be the gift of the anticipated limited lifespan. But then all these teasing questions and 'what ifs?' are part of what Michael O'Siadhail calls *The Long Apprenticeship of Assent*,[179] as accurate a title as any for my vocation to illness.

Public truth

By his wounds we are healed. (1 Peter 2.24)

After more than thirty years in England, my accent and surname still publicly mark me out as an 'Ulsterman of Planter Stock',[180] an obstinate race who like to argue and debate. I can still recall the 'rush' when making a speech about the IRA campaign in Ulster in the fifties when I was about ten years old! I am still energized by the preparation and the event of preaching even after forty years, Sunday by Sunday. So the seeds of my public ministry were sown early. It has been divided between adult/theological education and that of a parish priest. The common thread running through these two career paths is communication. I enjoy communicating and helping people to make sense of things. More than that I *seem* to need to communicate so that I can find out what I myself am thinking.

---

178 Popularly attributed to St Francis de Sales, Bishop of Geneva 1602–22, *Treatise on Divine Love*.

179 O'Siadhail, 'Threshold'.

180 John Hewitt in *The Irish Times* 4 July 1974: cited by Alan Warner in Alan Warner (ed.), *The Selected Poems of John Hewitt*, Blackstaff Press, 1981.

Making public sense of things cannot always be controlled and protected by the disciplines of pulpit, study or seminar. It is prey to all the risks of pastoral encounter. It is confusing, even threatening, to be moved in and out of role at the whim of a chance meeting or another's agenda. In this sense the professional obligation laid on me, as a publicly ill 'parson',[181] to offer public sense of my illness sometimes feels confusing and always threatening.

Confusion strikes when I start winding myself up for the monthly treatment at the hospital and I have to decide who 'I' am. On the morning of my hospital visit, I wake early before anyone else in the house. My first decision is over what to wear. Do I want to be privately or publicly ill today? Should I or should I not wear my 'uniform'. Do I have the energy to be the sick priest? Later I am put on the spot. Every month I am asked, 'What religion are you?' Do I say, 'None?' I can't say no if I have the collar on even if I feel particularly irreligious that day and can't cope with the accompanying expectations and projections. Priest or patient? Who am I today? One or the other? Can I be both? Being a professional wounded healer[182] never sits easy. I can cope with being a priest and being wounded now and again but certainly not all the time. Yet that was the ministry and cross of Christ. His wounds are healing for us. Writer and wounded pastor Henri Nouwen reminded us:

> The main question is not 'How can we hide our wounds?' so we don't have to be embarrassed, but 'How can we put our woundedness in the service of others?' When our wounds cease to be a source of shame, and become a source of healing, we have become wounded healers.[183]

---

181 'Parson' with the meaning of the representative person in community.

182 Isaiah's Suffering Servant; T. S. Eliot, 'East Coker', 'Four Quartets', in T. S. Eliot, *The Complete Poems and Plays*, Harcourt, Brace & World, 1962, p. 127. Henri Nouwen, *The Wounded Healer*, Doubleday New York & Co., 1972.

183 Nouwen, *The Wounded Healer*. Also cited in Will Hernandez, *A Spirituality of Imperfection*, Paulist, 2006, p. 116.

But is it not so much the *putting* (still implying control) as the *gifting* of our woundedness in the service of others?

Gifting my woundedness necessitated 'coming out' about my illness. I began the process by asking, who to tell and when? I was direct with most of the family (Diane, my wife, had accompanied me to the prognosis meeting with my consultant) but I made a decision to protect my ten-year-old daughter and my elderly mother. With my mother I was just vague, talking generally about a 'blood complaint'. I felt that our relationship would suffer less this way than if I had told her the full truth. Hindsight suggests that maternal instinct intuited knew more than I thought. My strategy backfired with my daughter. We were browsing in a bookshop one day and she caught me leafing through a book on cancer and immediately confronted me: 'Do you have cancer Dad?' It felt as if I had been caught leafing through a magazine from the top shelf, *flagrante delicto*. I had to own up. It has since proved to be a lesson in the benefits of coming out, for she is the one member of the family who asks the most direct and detailed questions about my state of health, absolutely refusing to be put off by my usual generalizations. Eight years later she applied to do Bio-Medical Sciences at University so, she said, that she could fully understand the nature of my illness. She seemed able to cope better than I did. Being candid was right for her, but perhaps not for everyone. How to distinguish one from the other was the hard part. One size doesn't fit all.

I *shared* my diagnosis with the wardens and with the verger who is the information hub of my largest parish. Bush telegraph did the rest. It felt odd, left-handed. Maybe this is a little of what lepers felt in the Bible. I certainly wasn't shunned, though for some 'it' wouldn't be mentioned. Offers of practical kindness poured in. Lift rotas for my journey to the hospital were spontaneously organized; the parish sent us on a wonderful holiday to Italy after a particularly bad spell, but most healing of all was knowing that prayers were being offered in the most unexpected quarters. My vulnerability seemed to make me more accessible, more emotionally available.

I *informed* the Bishop. He blew in, pronounced a blessing and left as quickly as he had come. That was his style. He told me that my illness was 'for the glory of God'. It was either a cryptic sort of comment or something that Bishops said to their sick clergy. Whichever, it was definitely a theological pronouncement which passed over my head. The visit was appreciated but, at the time, his words were a bad joke. However, in time, they pushed me, even goaded me to wrestle with the challenge of making sense of my illness from God's angle, his (patterned) side of the tapestry, to use a common metaphor. Certainly nothing seemed glorious about such a diagnosis and prognosis.

Years later I glimpsed the glory in a patient who came regularly for blood transfusions as her leukaemia had exhausted all treatment options. Sister Margaret Mary's glory, unheralded, was her ministry of quiet, purposeful befriendment. She had a gift for intuiting those who needed support and through her conversations, prayers and correspondence embodied the attractiveness of God's faithful love. I was one who was blessed by being 'found' by her. I recall phoning the convent when she was near to death and hearing the comforting reassurance that 'margaret Mary was being prayed into heaven'. Through her his Glory was shared and felt but not publicly named except by her 'uniform'. Unlike me, for her the vocation to public illness had been accepted and lived to the full. Her wounds were offered as healing for us. That was her glory.

I could see her illness was for the glory of God but how was mine? A possible beginning to an answer came right out of the blue one day from a friend who asked whether I was a better person because of my illness. Why did she ask? Did she recognize something about my public persona that I couldn't see? *I* certainly didn't feel a better person. Indeed I often felt a worse person and not fit to be in anyone's company. Paradoxically, during some periods of treatment I did feel more intensely alive and if 'the glory of God is a person fully alive'[184] then maybe, in that sense, I was a better person. More challenging is the need to recognize my 'anointing' as a patient/priest/parson[185] whose . . . real aim is not so much to see God in all things' as 'that God, through

184 Irenaeus, *Adversus Haereses* IV 34 5–7.

185 Irenaeus, *Adversus Haereses*.

us, should see the things that we see'.[186] That feels more active and vocationally direct like Kerry Hardie on Sheep Fair Day.[187]

Glimpses of glory are equally ambiguous in the daily round of pastoral work. I feel nakedly vulnerable when visiting the seriously ill. Before there was a sort of protective firewall, a detachment. Now my illness has switched off the firewall and the death virus is rampant. Now, sometimes depressingly, I am closer to people in their dying; sometimes too close for comfort. I buried the retired local police sergeant early in my time in the parish. J . . . was always circumspect about the nature of his chronic illness. All he would say was that he had to visit the hospital regularly to have his blood checked. I didn't realize at the time that we shared a similar diagnosis. His grave is on the other side of the path from the West Door, a constant personal reminder – 'dust thou art and to dust thou shalt return'.

Calling on parishioners with cancer inevitably resurrects those feelings. I feel an identity with them and they identify with me in a way that sometimes transmits itself as fellow-traveller but, more difficult, as projection on to me of places and depths where I have not been. So, visiting the acutely ill often feels like a case of mutual over identification and projection. And when an aggressive cancer takes a parishioner or colleague like A . . ., a reader with whom I worked, there is also the inevitable sense of survivor's guilt.

Despite these caveats I have come to the conclusion that the protective (professional?) firewall, behind which some of us pastors operate, is a hindrance. To acknowledge our own wounds is to offer hospitality for healing and to don the mantel of him

186 Janet Morley, citing Simone Weil, *The Heart's Time*, SPCK, 2012, p. 107.

187 Morley, *The Heart's Time*, Kerry Hardie:
I took God with me to the sheep fair. I said 'look,
There's Liv sitting on the wall, waiting;
These are pens, these are sheep . . .'

whose glorification was his lifting up on a cross so that 'by his wounds' (1 Peter 2.24) we all may be healed.

Present truth

Death is a lifetime's pilgrimage.[188]

This Monday is the beginning of treatment week. I have been to my local medical centre to have bloods taken and collect my monthly supply of pills and then on Thursday I have the three-monthly appointment with my consultant. Mortality looms large this week. The 'Departure Lounge', my treatment ward, is already beginning to induce black premonitions of finality and I am forcing myself to live only in the present, in transition from normal health to sickness . . . 'always a place where there's no company, where nobody can follow'.[189] And it is lonely.

This is me, terminally ill one day per month. Come this Saturday, if all goes well, I will be released (and it still feels like that) back into the company of the living. I will climb back up the ladder on the Snakes and Ladders board and resume the varied and satisfying way of life I will have had in the days prior to this week's treatment. Yesterday Madge (at whose wedding I had presided a couple of years ago) presented her son for baptism. She, Laurence and father Stewart, had come down from Shetland for the occasion and we all gathered afterwards in sunny spring weather at the village hall for a long champagne lunch and christening cake. Today I must also visit a former churchwarden seriously ill in hospital; tomorrow a Deanery Quiet Day and on Wednesday I am involved in the appointment of a teacher at one of the local schools. There is a satisfying feel of learning and urgency in our Lent groups. That is my portion, private invisible illness and public ministry in all its variety and richness.

---

188 Ambrose (fourth-century Bishop of Milan), 'Treatise on the Blessings of Death', in Brother Kenneth Collins (ed.), *From the Fathers to the Churches*, HarperCollins, 2003, p. 169.

189 Ellsberg, *The Saints' Guide*, p. 119.

Learning to inhabit this mix of life and death is my 'long apprenticeship of assent'; my trusted tool is seventeenth-century poet Richard Crashaw's prayer:[190]

> Still live in me this loving strife
> Of living death and dying life.

My hope is that this account should not seem negative but suggest the possibility of a *loving strife*; not just an assent to death but a befriending of it and an opportunity to 'learn that it is a trustful giving place'.[191]

Postscript

My father was a priest in the Church of Ireland. He died of a brain tumour when he was fifty-eight and I was sixteen. I was the last of my family to see him alive. That his illness was 'a death long in dying'[192] has echoed loudly in my mind down the years. My illness has gifted me an unsuspected and precious legacy. It is the acknowledgement that my father, with whom I never had an adult relationship, actually walked this same road. I walk *with* him now, not as a child but as an adult. At times I like to think of my leukaemia as being, yes, 'a death long in dying', but also as an intimation of that longed for man to man 'conversation', the sort I never had with him. Those gnawing persistent questions of God's call and purposes are not just mine but more intimately 'ours'. We really do share a vocation. My illness has released me to 'put away childish things'. I am growing up.

190 Richard Crashaw, 'A Song', in George Walton Williams (ed.), *Complete Works of Richard Crashaw*, Doubleday, 1970, p. 65. Also cited in Peter Coughlan, Ronald Jasper and Teresa Rodrigues, *A Christian's Prayer Book*, Geoffrey Chapman, 1974, p. 142.

191 Rowan Williams, 'University Sermon' preached at University Church of St Mary the Virgin, Oxford, 29 November 1987.

192 Lancelot Andrewes, 'A Sermon preached on Good Friday 1605', in Collins, *From the Fathers to the Church*, p. 500.

11

Dark before Dawn

RACHEL LEWIS

Unusually, the rest of the family were working away, so it was a relatively peaceful week before Christmas when I found a tiny lump and went for a reassuring appointment with my GP. 'Before I examine you,' she began,' I want you to know that I will be sending you to the Breast Care clinic for follow-up tests whatever we think it might be. I send all my ladies.' Her smile was warm, her advice was encouraging. 'It looks like a cyst to me, but we need to be sure. Don't worry though, given your family history you really are a very low risk.' I registered what she said, and felt reassured. I knew about cysts – odd lumps or bumps that become benign friends.

My clinic appointment was two days later, 23 December 2002. It was the day my husband was coming home, as were quite a lot of the family who were joining us for the holiday. Those last precious Advent days are always busy for parish priests – busy for everyone with school and community excitements. By good fortune my appointment was set for a time after the Red Cross Christmas lunch and before our eagerly anticipated family dinner that evening. Even if I had to wait to be seen, there would be time when I got home to get ready. The family is used to my being out for most of the day at this time of year, and was, in any case, happily unpacking, swapping news and surreptitiously hiding brightly coloured parcels as I left the house. I didn't think to tell them anything, they were busy and excitedly catching up and there seemed to be no need to worry them when there might be nothing to worry about.

Mammograms are not dignified or comfortable, but the nurse was as gentle as she could be. She was kind and funny too, which always makes you feel more human. 'Just go back and wait by the water cooler and we'll find you to let you know the result,' she said. After a while – long enough to read through my plans for the crib service and sermon notes for midnight communion – I was invited into another small office to hear the results from the man who was to become my new best friend.

I don't remember the actual words he used to explain what my X-ray told them. I do remember him saying, 'That's very bad', as he pointed to three tiny dark splodges on the transparency. 'But try not to worry. We'll just take a biopsy to find out more. Come back for the results on 2 January. Sorry it'll take a little bit longer than we'd like, it's because of the bank holidays.' They were kind too, the nurse holding my hand tight as he took a biopsy. I didn't look, even though I'm not funny about needles. After I'd dressed again, I waited to hear more instructions. 'Try to put this to the back of your mind and enjoy Christmas. We'll see you again on the second,' Mr Collins said, while he wrote on the back of an envelope, 'DRIVE VERY CAREFULLY'. They had clearly broken this sort of news before.

We did enjoy Christmas and I didn't share my worry. I did, in fact seem to forget about it. After all, nothing was hurting, my energy was good and the Advent hope *was* realized in the most tremendous tale of all, where 'the maker of the stars and sea became a child on earth for me'.[192] In retrospect, I imagine that it was the mind's way of coping with the shock and the uncertainty. The waiting. Besides which, there isn't a great deal of time to worry with the full-on public role of leading Christmas worship and celebrations in a group of five churches. Being surrounded by family and trying to maximize the short time we had together before they had to go home absorbed my full attention. It was the best Christmas we'd had.

January wasn't great and it got worse before it got better. It wasn't that I lacked distractions or that I relinquished my public responsibility of the privilege and joy of ministry over

192 John Betjeman, 'Christmas', *Collected Poems*, John Murray, 1951.

Christmas. It's that the human process of waiting for and then hearing bad news is difficult. Work has been done elsewhere on the physical and mental effects of shock, which I won't rehearse here. Besides, so many people have had to live through that unsettling process of waiting for test results. They still do. Universally, yet uniquely distressing, the dread feeling of being out of control; of not knowing, brings its own hell. And it seems to me that priests (and those who love them) don't have an easier time of it when it happens to them.

So, what was it like for me and mine? The honest answer is that it was very hard. Life became hard when the bad news was public, shared. It was as though the spotlight of others' shock and concern suddenly came rushing in. But, I trust in God and know that I am in safe hands, irrespective of whatever happens. Having given any concern for my future over to him while I did my clerical duty (and joy) over Christmas, in the midst of the good time we were all having there didn't seem to be a good time to share any possible concern with my nearest and dearest. However, being alone with my husband on New Year's Day precipitated the sharing of the unknown state of my health and our future. I don't know if there *is* a good way to let someone know that you may have cancer, but if there is one I didn't find it. I know that cancer and the name of someone you love shouldn't be in the same sentence, let alone in the same body. But here, it was. Cancer was in my body. Tough to say and tough to hear. So, we walked. Not talking, just walking and walking and walking along the parallel tracks of the deserted railway lines, wrapped up in scarves against the biting wind. Initially, especially before the surgery and subsequent scans revealed more precisely the limit of the cancer, there is understandably a good deal of fear. One's thoughts aren't easy to control when one's next visit to the doctor might mean a death sentence. There seems to be only bad language to use.

The next day we went to get the results together. The medical staff were as kind as before. For me, it seemed quite straightforward to hear that for my type of cancer I should go for surgery a week on Monday. After the mastectomy I would be seeing another specialist about my chemotherapy. They explained at length, not that I remembered the details of what they said and I don't think that Richard even heard that they were talking. It was the last time he was wobbly though, from there on in he was as firm as St Peter himself; clear that I would be treated and that I would be fixed. And I was.

Wales, where my family lived, is a long way from where we were living in County Limerick, so telling them my news over the phone was difficult. I realize that for them, hearing the news over the phone felt worse. However, they were determinedly bright and positive in their responses and swung into immediate action with aplomb. Mother, also a priest, promised to get the good pray-ers onto my case. 'No learners,' she assured me. 'We need to batter the heavens on your behalf.' True to her word she canvassed the prayerful support of every Archbishop, Bishop, Rabbi, and spiritual heavyweight that she could think of. For this, and for all their prayers I am eternally grateful. My sister knew a lot of breast-care specialists through her work and her job was to 'find stuff out'. The others simply sent love in their own way; some with texts and jokes, others with cards and phone messages 'for no good reason at all'. We are richly blessed and upheld in love in all sorts of shapes. Parishioners and friends were solid gold in their appropriate care and support. Besides their private and public prayers, I received cards, flowers and phone messages. Importantly, they kept in touch with those closest to me separately, which was a significant generous support that I only learned about later.

We came to realize realities that had been abstract theories before my illness. Faith and hope flooded in. I came to know existentially that life is fragile, that health is precious, and that it's to be appreciated rather than taken for granted. And love flooded in. Family and friends are mostly taken for granted when we are strong, seemingly bombproof. In the midst of realizing our own frailty it was a blessing to realize how deep a grace family and friendship are. Writings that I held in my 'treasure chest' became startlingly real. I felt the care and compassion of Christ through the hands and eyes of others:[193]

Christ has no body but yours,
No hands, no feet on earth but yours,
Yours are the eyes with which he looks
Compassion on this world.

There were to be many occasions during my surgery and treatment when this touched me deeply. The night before surgery I was in my hospital bed with the screens drawn around me. I had understood their warnings that my surgery was major and, as with any general anaesthetic, there was a danger of death. I had signed the relevant paperwork. I had been weighed, measured, tested and X-rayed; bloods had been taken and date of birth, name and address checked often. I had been given a pre 'pre-med' to help me sleep and knew that I would be taken to theatre first thing in the morning. I wasn't as calm as I had been up until then, and my attention butterflied frustratingly from the book I had taken in to calm my nerves. A colleague asked me subsequently if I had prayed as Jesus did in Gethsemane, 'let this cup pass from me'. If I did, then I don't remember doing so. In my memory, the significant prayer before the mastectomy operation was Matthews' prayer following a sudden shock:[194]

Gatherer of Souls, draw to me my scattered soul,
May no part be lost, May no part be straying.
Preserve my soul in peace in the soul-shrine of my body.

The phrase that gave me strength, that gently helped me breathe was: 'May no part be lost, May no part be straying. Preserve my soul in peace . . .' The idea that the scattered patches of my soul were safe soothed me. Let no part of me be lost, lonely or afraid. Other quieting thoughts echoing that same plea came

193 Attributed to Teresa of Avila.

194 Caitlin Matthews, *The Celtic Devotional: Daily prayers and Blessings*, Godsfield, 1996, p. 127.

from snatches of prayers known by heart. Some of them are so deeply embedded that it was as though they glowed in my consciousness like a night light for small children. Prayers that have been heartbeat close since birth and possibly from the womb, including the night prayer:

> Save us, O Lord, while waking and guard us while sleeping, that awake we may watch with Christ and asleep we may rest in peace.[195]

Other threads of trusted safety-net woven around me were provided by those who held me in their prayers privately and publicly. Akin to knowing myself to be 'surrounded by so great a cloud of witnesses' (Hebrews 12.1). I now know that I was held within a giant and wonderful wave of prayerful support, which was an extraordinarily powerful force for good in my healing and recovery. In the same way as the surgeons and medical professionals did their job in cutting and pasting my body together to remove the cancer, it was for other people to do the praying on my behalf as for me the words evaded me like fish in a river. My role was to keep breathing and receiving and growing stronger. Healing or letting myself be healed.

My own thoughts now are that I was in no position to think about or talk with God other than through those snap-shot sentences. Other people were doing that for me. It was their job. My job was to keep breathing and to trust. Whatever happened the busy-ness of my mind calmed. I was not afraid to die.

I came round from the anaesthetic heavily bandaged and groggy. One of my first visitors was my consultant surgeon, who assured me that the surgery had gone very well. 'Just remember,' he told me, 'you're injured. You're not sick, you're injured.' To have been given that distinction to keep in my mind helped me heal quickly. And I did. I believe and trust that they removed the cancer, they had found no spread in the lymph nodes they had taken from my armpit, and I was fixed. It took a

195 *Common Worship, Night Prayer.*

couple of deep breaths to get used to looking at the place where my breast used to be and to let others look at the place too, but, thank God, bodies are fascinating and quite amazing, as are our hearts and minds.

Thank God too for the dedicated breast-care nurses for the fitting of my mastectomy bras and silicone prosthesis and for their grounded sense of humour. What has this to do with God? Back to Teresa of Avila; it has everything to do with the generosity and appropriate nature of care that was shown to me and to the family. The nurses spent over half an hour to balance me up because, as they told me, 'If you think anyone is going to be looking you in the eye for the next six months you're wrong – they'll be looking to see which one you've had taken away.'

Chemotherapy would follow soon with the upside of meeting a fabulous hairdresser. Hair is funny stuff. It shouldn't matter much, but it actually matters intensely. My coiffure shrank from 'oh-so pampered' long hair, to a shorter cut, until there was nothing else for it but to ask Cyril to take me under his wing for the practicalities of a therapeutic wig. So, as my hair fell out and thinned alarmingly, but before it straggled into complete baldness, Cyril buzzed what remained to within half an inch of my skull, harmlessly flirting with me as he did so. Just what I needed, probably above and beyond the call of duty but I did so appreciate his kindness. When history tells us that to shave a woman's head is a deliberately degrading action, his humour and attention held me above those particular depths of despair. Luckily I discovered that my head isn't shaped like a ping-pong ball, and the funky close crop suited me. A significant confidence booster in the midst of the horrible physical reactions to the poison that was curing me by killing the cancer. Positive surprises mattered deeply. The amazing feel of the weather on my head! Breezes, raindrops, sunshine heat.

This change of appearance had happened very soon after my first session of chemotherapy. I was due to have six, but in the end I had only two, and the following will explain why. In our first meeting the oncologist confirmed that the surgery had removed the cancer. I was clear. All the tests corroborated that truth. He told us that the chemotherapy was 'more or less belt and braces, just to be on the safe side'. I hadn't known much about chemotherapy before, but I soon learned that, for me at least, it involved lengthy stretches of time in a well-appointed clinic to have various chemicals slowly injected into the veins of my right hand and arm. Due to the surgery my left hand and arm were no longer to be used for bloods or blood pressure checks – ever. It was to do with not compromising the limb. So, the veins of my right arm were used for the injections. Chemotherapy can have a brutal effect on your body (it's meant to I guess). The veins in my arm collapsed after the second session, and so did I. I didn't know about either of these facts for a good while – I simply 'moved into another room'.[196]

This physical collapse following my second session of chemotherapy brought peace and freedom into rest and love for me. For the family who found me, panic; and confusion for the doctors who needed to determine why I had slipped into this coma. Had the cancer spread to my brain? Had they missed something?

Frustratingly, I only know what I have been told by others about this episode, and no one told me very much despite my badgering them. This is all I know.

Seemingly, we were back to the amazing creation that our bodies are with their fine and vulnerable balance of salts and fluids. The chemotherapy had thrown these into a mess, and I had acute hydronatremia, or 'a low sodium reaction'. My body couldn't cope, so it went into a coma for a day or so. I learned later that when they did realize how to sort me out, I recovered very quickly. I woke to hear a woman calling me by name and asking me if I knew where I was. I didn't, nor did I recognize the nightdress I was wearing. Perhaps I was dreaming. 'You're in hospital.' The reality that I wasn't dreaming became clearer as my thoughts came back and I realized that I had an almighty headache. This was to last a long time – months.

---

196 Henry Scott Holland, 'Funeral', in Daisy Goodwin (ed.), *101 Poems that could Save your Life*, HarperCollins, 2003.

What I do remember is that somehow I realized, I knew that I had to come back from my blissful experience to real life, which would involve pain and struggle and weakness and brokenness and time in the mending.

We live our lives forward but understand them backwards, so that much of what follows is a mixture of what I wrote in my diaries and how I have reflected on the episode since.

To know the blissful love which is death – no, that's wrong. I knew a blissful love which came with a release from conscious life for a while, because I did not die. To have known this blissful love is to understand a little of the blessing, essential, generous nature of sleep, rest and forgiveness. Release from weariness, stress, guilt or anxiety. Release from pain. I felt released into love. I don't remember a particular light or specific people around me, simply that generous sensation of unconditional love. It is what I now think of when I read about love stronger than death, lasting into eternity at a funeral service. Love IS stronger than death. Love which doesn't depend on physical ability or gesture, but a love which grows from the spirit within a person. To me, that in turn, is rooted and grounded in God. The Comforter, 'the fruit of the spirit of truth (bringing) all the attendant gifts of love, joy, peace, patience, kindness, generosity, faithfulness, gentleness and self-control' (Galatians 5.22–3). It is love; not sentimental love, but diamond love; catching and reflecting the brilliance of the light of the world. Backbone-of-steel love. Since regaining consciousness and 'coming back to the real world' I know and am blessed still to know this to be true in the depths of my soul.

This is not to say that ever since then my life was, has been or is pain or trouble free. Far from it. But I thank God for the gift of deeper knowledge of my own body and soul. My self as loved and gathered into that love which is immortal. The perfect love which casts out all fear. We know and trust this to be true through God's word and God's grace. We know from scripture that God is love. We know that God loved the world so much that he became human. Holding John 1.1 in my heart I journalled:

> Love became; took flesh.
> Love found voice and told us how to love.
> Love found friends and showed us how to love.
>
> The night before he died
> he took a towel and a bowl of water
> and washed their feet.
>
> 'Do this,' he told his friends.
>
> Love serves.
>
> Love opens its arms, opens its heart.
> Arms open to be broken with nails.
> Hearts open to be broken; and opened to be broken; and opened again . . .

'Love, like fire, can only reveal its brightness in the failure and the beauty of burnt wood.'[197] We know that for many the crucifixion was considered as failure, an ignominious defeat. Jesus died a cruelly painful, publicly shaming death. His followers had betrayed him and left him. Those who believe the Christian gospel believe that this was not a plan gone wrong, but a plan fulfilled. God chose what was weak to shame the strong. And, if God really is God, as he is revealed in the life and teaching of Jesus, then God knows, and God loves and God forgives.[198]

Human bodies are as fragile as the dark before the dawn. Such benediction is truly a mystery. Echoes reach us from unexpected parts of our life journey, and one such is R. S. Thomas's poem,

---

197 John O'Donahue, *Conamara Blues*, Bantam Books, 2001, p. 53.

198 From my notes taken during Bishop David Jenkins' keynote address, 'Council 2000', Yatton Keynell, 1998.

'The Musician'.[199] When I was in my teens I was a dedicated, though terrified piano soloist. Before a particularly grand concert, my music teacher gave me a copy of this poem, I suppose to reassure me. Then the words that stayed with me concerned the physical performance of the musician, Fritz Kreisler.

> I could see, too, the twitching of the fingers,
> Caught temporarily in art's neurosis,
> As we sat there or warmly applauded
> This player who so beautifully suffered
> For each of us upon his instrument.

Now, years later and in a different public context, it was the words from the last verse which resonated. They describe the man, Jesus, on Calvary:

> Making such music as lives still.
> And no one daring to interrupt
> Because it was himself that he played
> And closer than all of them the God listened.

In the 1980s there was a campaign to raise awareness of global solidarity with those living with HIV/AIDS in Africa. 'The body of Christ has Aids' served as an arresting call to us who are connected in the Body of Christ to share in and respond to their suffering. Today it feels as though the Body of Christ has Cancer. So many of us live closely to this disease. While I do believe that cancer should not be in the same sentence let alone the same body as someone you love, it does – very often. At the time I went through my treatment one in eight people would be treated for breast cancer in Ireland. Perhaps because I was going through this, or perhaps for a completely different reason, I found many conversations included experiences of cancer one way or another. A colleague (from South Africa originally) talked about having had a double mastectomy. 'No

---

199 R. S. Thomas, *Tares*, Chester Springs, 1961.

one notices,' she said, 'except on the beach. It's not pretty but I'm not vain, besides beaches here aren't warm enough for me to take my shirt off.' The mother of three children in the Sunday School simply shared, 'I expect to have cancer some time – we all will.' It was clear from her attitude, that the disease would be sorted. Managed, or fixed; a chronic disease.

Talking about cancer is becoming ordinary, which is a good thing. No longer are we in fear to speak in euphemisms: 'the big "C"'. Naming the disease serves to take some of the fear away, relieve the isolation. As a Lutheran priest friend said, 'I had my cancer five years ago – ovarian – not long before we adopted the girls.' She sent me a copy of this poem, which has become widely familiar, though the author is unknown.

Cancer is so limited
It cannot cripple love.
It cannot shatter hope.
It cannot corrode faith.
It cannot eat away peace.
It cannot destroy confidence.
It cannot shut out memories.
It cannot silence courage.
It cannot invade the soul.
It cannot steal eternal life.
It cannot conquer the spirit.
Cancer is so limited.

The body of Christ has cancer. And all shall be well. As my strength grew and my energy returned, there were two public speaking engagements which were significant. The first was to introduce a report in the Diocesan Synod AGM about being church in the twenty-first century. Before the report proper, I thanked everyone for their prayerful support of me and of the family through my surgery and treatment as this had been so important in my recovery. I talked about St Paul's comments, that an ear is an ear and not an eye and eyes are eyes and can't hear (1 Corinthians 12.17–9), then told them that my plastic surgeon had told me that a tummy could become a breast, whatever St Paul would have had to say about that! The point I was trying to make that we need not to be afraid of doing things differently when they go wrong. Change can be healing, strong and good.

The second talk was a five-minute 'gentle reminder' to a group of ladies at a breast cancer charity fashion show. Introduced as someone who was 'in remission' (and there I was thinking I was fixed!). In my five minutes, I told my story with its good bits and bad bits, but mostly the funny bits. At the end I was stunned and embarrassed to be given a standing ovation, only to get back to my seat and have my fellow speaker, the consultant breast surgeon confide to me, 'They always do that to survivors.' And maybe they do in recognition of the speech made; stand for the speaker. But I think that they stand up for themselves, out of respect and relief at human resilience. A standing ovation for being alive. Corporately.

We are, as the psalmist wrote:

> fearfully and wonderfully made. You created my inmost being; you knit me together in my mother's womb . . . wonderful are your works; I know that very well. (Psalm 139.13–14)

Since then, I have undergone further surgery for reconstruction, and am now back to my old self. Or rather my new self. Skilled and patient surgeons spent over six hours cutting and sewing me together into shape. Psalm 139 sang out through all that the surgeons and other healthcare professionals were able to do. I am fearfully and wonderfully remade. Our bodies are our main way of experiencing God's goodness, love, purpose and grace. Realization of these things grew as my recovery and rebuilding of self grew, with confidence in my personal role as daughter, wife and friend, alongside my public, representative role as spiritual leader. Biblical role models helped too, some surprisingly. In this category I put Peter's mother-in-law. My instinct is that for her to get up from her sick bed and immediately serve others was to fulfil expectations of a society which went too far – it was she who should have been ministered to. Perhaps I am mellowed with age, but I now feel that this miracle can be looked at differently. In healing her this way, Jesus restored her to what gave her worth (whatever our modern offence at that). I now know deeply how important it is for us to know that we have the health, strength and opportunity to serve as well as receive the service of others.

More informal recovery and fun came through joining a Patchwork group in Limerick. The creative company, making new friendships with much laughter, became important. The process of making patchwork pieces gave me enough focus for my hands and eyes, while my thoughts could play with ideas. For instance, what does it mean to be rearranged a bit like a piece of patchwork – all those left-over bits of fabric? Some from the past, some from now, colours and textures forgotten and put together into something new. There is the aspect of cutting up perfectly good fabric and putting the bits together in a new way. Re-building and remembering, have been significant recurring ideas that I have used in my sermons and reflections over the years about community, the Eucharist, continuity, reconciliation. One morning my spiritual reflection gave the thought for the day as 'the compassion of memory'. Memory. Remembering. Re-membering. Deliberately recalling and then staying with particular memories. Using them to shape or perhaps reshape present understanding of situations and relationships in order better to appreciate and resource future vision and plans. Compassion has a sympathetic quality. It is healing, restoring. To think of memory through this lens was useful. What did the past bring with compassion to the now? Strength, creativity, energy, risk and delight. Sadness, pain, loneliness, despair – memories all jumbled up over the years. Selective reflection is the prerogative of the thinker, of course, to choose only the positive and wholesome. But not all memories are. What is the compassionate nature of pain or frustration or of destructive feelings and patterns. Perhaps it is for those feelings to evoke compassionate response from the now; to re-member the memory. Healing backwards.

Before I lived through my cancer, I mainly enjoyed the stress of busy parochial life and bustle. But I wouldn't be honest if I did not confess that there were times when I knew that I was driving myself too hard – overextending my energy, overworking my strength in order to meet deadlines. Like many of us I would often reach the end of a day and pray, rather grandly echoing the prayer of Augustine that God would slow me down but not yet.

No one expects to be slowed by a diagnosis of cancer and I was no exception. But slow me down it most surely did. The experience taught me many lessons, most importantly, that every precious day of life that we wake is a blessing. How we live out that day in the best way that we can matters. Life is a gift. Since coming back into harness, the full-on, full-time ministry of parochial life, I have been signed off by the medical specialists, with only the usual health checks and monitoring. In my writing from those years and since, I have reflected on how I hoped to have the strength not to return to my former too-busy life pattern; grateful to have dodged a bullet; mindful of the miracle that was my healing. I pray that I shall continue to do so while I have health and strength and breath.

12

Lament

GORDON MURSELL

> A theology engaged with the prophets, the wisdom writings, the Psalms, and the Gospels will value questioning. One thinks of the medieval scholastic insistence on the *quaestio* and the dialectic of argument that culminated in the theology of Thomas Aquinas – a new tradition inculcating rigorous debate. Modern thinkers have often directed hostile questioning of extreme suspicion and scepticism against Christian faith from the outside, but it may be the insiders who have asked the most disturbing questions – Martin Luther, Søren Kierkegaard, or Donald MacKinnon. Few Christians who have access to the best thinkers on both sides tend to find themselves convinced by the arguments of anti-Christians – there are usually rebuttals by Christians who are at least as intelligent, educated and rationally persuasive as their opponents . . . God's questioning, as in the prophets, Job, and Jesus, turns out to be more dangerous than any of those who try to explain God away, and it by no means excludes terrible doubt and wrestling with God. The wisdom of interrogation and dispute that is so vital to Christian theological existence includes dispute about and with God.[200]

These reflections by the Cambridge theologian David Ford may cause some surprise to believers and non-believers alike. They

200 David Ford, *The Future of Christian Theology*, Wiley-Blackwell, 2011, p. 77.

shouldn't: honest questioning is as central to religious faith as it is to science. Like everyone else, people of faith have to live with doubt and fear and suffering. Their faith does not insure them against these things: perhaps what it does is to provide a different perspective in which to view them, a different layout of emotional and spiritual furniture in which to inhabit them. And this will not be easy, especially (though not only) for those who hold some public or representative role within the faith community, such as the contributors to this book. The conflict – or rather the *collision* – between public persona and private faith can be desperately hard to endure, let alone to make sense of.

There is nothing new about this. The Gospels tell the story of Jairus, a prominent public figure in the local Galilean synagogue, with a private sorrow: his daughter is dying. He does not, or cannot, manage this sorrow alone: he brings it to Jesus. Too late, as it seems: by the time Jesus responds, the little girl is dead. Yet it is not too late: Jesus says to Jairus, 'Do not fear, only believe' (Mark 5.21–34). And the girl's life is restored.[201] It's worth noting that the act of restoration is not described as depending on Jairus' faith: it was his despair, not his faith, that drove him to Jesus in the first place. Even so, as the contributors to this book demonstrate, Jesus' instruction not to fear but only to believe is easier said than done. They, and we, may identify with another character in the Gospels, another parent with a child who is critically ill, who cries out to Jesus, 'I believe; help my unbelief' (Mark 9.24).

How do we cope when faith and experience collide painfully, when the chasm between our public persona and private anguish appears unbridgeable? For some, the spirituality of Psalm 131 offers hope in the honest recognition that we are not in control of much of what happens to us, and the handing over to a loving God in childlike trust:

> O Lord, my heart is not lifted up,
> my eyes are not raised too high;
> I do not occupy myself with things

201 In Matthew's version of the story (9.18–26), the little girl is dead even before Jairus meets Jesus.

too great and too marvellous for me.
But I have calmed and quieted my soul,
like a weaned child with its mother;
my soul is like the weaned child that is with me.[202]
O Israel, hope in the Lord
from this time on and forevermore.

Read in the context of Jane Tillier's reflections on the experience of multiple miscarriages, this prayer becomes almost unbearably moving. But it also makes powerful sense as the prayer of someone in a position of responsibility who is acutely aware of the gap between the public rôle and the sense of inner inadequacy. As so often in the Psalms, the focus moves from the individual to the community when, in the final verse, the psalmist moves from prayer to exhortation, from addressing God to encouraging the people of God to make his or her childlike trust their own.

For others, though, this is simply too cosy to work: something is needed that acknowledges more directly the dissonance between expectation and reality, between what we'd planned for our lives and what actually happens. At such times, and since time immemorial, human beings have turned to lament – and not just human beings; for lament is a creature's articulation of how it feels when suffering strikes, unlooked-for and undeserved, and the cry of an animal in pain is no less a lament than the more self-conscious expressions of it in art, poetry, drama, dance or music.[203]

202 Or 'my soul within me is like a weaned child' (NRSV footnote). Both translations are slightly conjectural: John Goldingay suggests, 'like one nursed with its mother, so is my spirit nursed with me', *Psalms Volume 3: Psalms 90–150*, Baker Academic, 2008, p. 533.

203 The second-century Christian writer Tertullian wrote: 'the whole creation prays. Cattle and wild beasts pray, and bend their knees, and in coming forth from their stalls and lairs look up to heaven, their mouth not idle, making the spirit move in their own fashion. Moreover the birds taking flight lift themselves up to heaven and instead of hands spread out the cross of their wings, while saying something which may be supposed to be a prayer', *On Prayer* 28–9, in the Roman *Divine Office* II, 1974, pp. 163–4.

For human beings, such art can accurately articulate, and give meaning to, the otherwise chaotic and meaningless depths of suffering and sorrow liable to overwhelm us if some kind of meaning cannot be found. Music is full of examples of lament, from the inexpressibly moving way in which ancient plainchant (free of the tight controls of tonality and rhythm) can add immense resonance and depth to the words of a psalm, to the late symphonies and string quartets of the Russian composer Dmitri Shostakovich, who struggled to find meaning and purpose in the almost unimaginable atmosphere of fear that pervaded his country during Stalin's rule: to listen to his Eighth Symphony, a threnody for the victims of the Second World War, is an extraordinarily cathartic experience even for those who have never known war. In 1991, the Scottish Catholic composer James MacMillan wrote *Tuireadh* (the Gaelic word for lament) for clarinet and string quartet, in which he sought to articulate the grief of the survivors and the bereaved from the Piper Alpha oil-rig disaster in the North Sea: he was 'particularly moved' by a letter sent to him by the mother of one of the Piper Alpha victims: describing the memorial service held at the scene of the tragedy, she told how 'a spontaneous keening sound rose gently from the mourners assembled on the boat'.[204] MacMillan's piece is full of this sound; and the piece as a whole evokes the astonishing words from the prophecy of Jeremiah, where it is God who laments:

> Consider, and call for the mourning women to come;
> send for the skilled women to come;
> let them quickly raise a dirge over us,
> so that our eyes may run down with tears . . . (Jeremiah 9.17–18)[205]

---

204 Stephen Johnson, in the notes to the CD recording of James MacMillan's *Tuireadh*, BIS-CD-1269.

205 The extended passage from Jeremiah 8.18–9.11 also makes most sense as God's lament over the fate of the people of Israel.

In traditional cultures, lament was often entrusted to women. The Irish writer J. M. Synge writes of his experience of it on the Aran Islands, off the west coast of Ireland:

> The grief of the keen is no personal complaint for the death of one woman over eighty years, but seems to contain the whole passionate rage that lurks somewhere in every native of the island. In this cry of pain the inner consciousness of the people seems to lay itself bare for an instant, and to reveal the mood of beings who feel their isolation in the face of a universe that wars on them with winds and seas. They are usually silent, but in the presence of death all outward show of indifference or patience is forgotten, and they shriek with pitiable despair before the horror of the fate to which they all are doomed.[206]

But for those for whom western classical music offers meaning and inspiration, the articulation of lament in the works of Johann Sebastian Bach may resonate most deeply. In his *Matthaüs-Passion*, Passion According to Matthew, Bach invites us to reflect on the Gospel's account of Jesus' arrest, trial and crucifixion on three different levels: first, there is the biblical text itself, sung with intense drama and feeling but without further interpretation or gloss; second, there are the arias, in which individual singers ponder, in both words and music, the impact of the Bible story for each one of those listening: what does this mean for me, now? Third, there are the hymns or chorales, sung either by the congregation or chorus, in which the community of faith appropriate for themselves the truth and significance of what they have heard. When the evangelist has sung the account of Jesus' arrest in Gethsemane, there follows what sounds like a sad and gentle aria for soprano and alto: '*So ist mein Jesus nun gefangen*' ('My Jesus is now captured, then'). But it is constantly interrupted by cries of lament from

---

206 From J. M. Synge, *The Aran islands* 1 1907 – accessible online at www.online-literature.com/synge/aran-islands/1.

the chorus: '*Lasst ihn, haltet, binden nicht!*' ('Leave him, stop, do not bind him!'); and when the two soloists sing with melancholy restraint '*Sie führen ihn, er ist gebunden*' ('They lead him away; he is bound'), the two choirs burst into the music, sweeping away the soloists' pious grieving in words and music of astonishing rage:

Sind Blitze, sind Donner in Wolken verschwunden?	Are lightning and thunder vanished in clouds?
Eröffne den feurigen Abgrund, o Hölle	Open up the fiery bottomless pit, O hell;
Zertrümmre, verderbe, verschlinge, zerschelle	Smash, ruin, swallow up, break to pieces
Mit plötzlicher Wut	With sudden fury
Den falschen Verräter, das mördrische Blut!	That false betrayer, That murderous blood![207]

Notice the 'that' – '*that* false betrayer, *that* murderous blood!' This tremendous aria articulates our outrage at such an act of betrayal, but leaves the blame for Jesus' death 'out there', on the convenient scapegoat of Judas Iscariot. Bach is not finished, however. After another short piece of scripture describing the disciples forsaking Jesus and fleeing, the first half of the St Matthew Passion ends with the monumental chorus: '*O Mensch, bewein' dein' Sünde gross*' ('O humankind, bewail your great sin'). In other words, the appalling and unjust execution of an innocent victim is the fault of his betrayer, who deserves ultimate retribution. But his betrayer is not just Judas: it is we who are responsible. Our individual and corporate guilt crucified the Son of God.

It is not only the western classical tradition of music that offers numerous examples of lament. Traditional folk song is full of it, from the spirituals of Afro-American slaves, or the

207 The English translation is taken from Michael Marissen, *Bach's Oratorios: The Parallel German-English Texts with Annotations*, Oxford University Press, 2008.

haunting Gaelic songs of Scottish crofters driven from their land during the infamous clearances, to the songs of Aztec poets from Mexico (the *Cantares Mexicanos* of 1523) crying out to God at the horror of the Spanish conquest of their country.[208] So is modern popular music: the Welsh singer Duffy established her reputation with songs such as 'Mercy' and 'Breaking My Own Heart', where the characteristics of lament – vivid articulations of despair and loss, combined with cries for deliverance and rescue, and urgent questioning of why such things have happened – are allowed full rein. Some musical laments (such as the music of Shostakovich) are not addressed to any God; but all of them can help the person who is suffering, whether adhering to any faith or none, to find hope and meaning in the heart of pain.

Within the Judaeo-Christian spiritual tradition, lament is supremely to be found in the book of Lamentations, in some of the great prophetic texts such as Isaiah and Jeremiah, in the book of Job and in the Psalms; and in these texts it usually takes the form of prayer. There is nothing inherently surprising about this: the pagan Roman poet Ovid, exiled to a bleak outpost of the Empire far from home, found (as so many since have done) that in moments of extreme despair only the language of prayer is available to do justice to what had happened to him: 'O gods of sea and sky – for what but prayer is left? – don't break the frame of our shattered boat.'[209] And innumerable people of little or no religious faith will, like Ovid, have turned to prayer at moments of crisis. It is precisely the way in which the Psalms, in particular, interweave prayer with personal reflection, denunciation of powerful enemies, or exhortation to

208 For black spirituals, see Jon Michael Spencer, *Protest and Praise: Sacred Music of Black Religion*, Augsburg Fortress, 1990. For Gaelic laments, see Anne Lorne Gillies, *Songs of Gaelic Scotland*, Birlinn, 2010. For the Aztec laments, see Migel León-Portilla (ed.), *The Broken Spears: The Aztec Account of the Conquest of Mexico*, Beacon, 1962, new ed. 1992, esp. pp. 145–9.

209 *Di maris et caeli – quid enim nisi vota supersunt? – solvere quassatae parcite membra ratis*, Ovid, Tristia I.2, lines 1–2.

others, which underlines their continuing power and relevance in an increasingly secular society.

It may help to look briefly at one example. Psalm 22 has become famous in Christian tradition because its opening words. 'My God, my God, why have you forsaken me?' are said by the Gospel writers to have been used by Jesus as he hung dying on the cross.[210] Any devout Jew might have recourse to their own scriptures at such moments, not only to find words that unlock the feelings and articulate the anguish within, but also to be reminded that others have trodden this path before them. And the Gospel writers discovered many things in this great prayer of lament which could help them make sense of Jesus' death, such as the words, 'He trusted in God; let God deliver him now, if he wants to', and the vivid description of the psalmist's clothes being divided as the jeering onlookers cast lots for them.[211] If we read the Psalm as the prayer of Jesus, it can help us to enter more deeply into the mystery of his suffering: its sharply contrasting moods, moving from agonized and lonely doubt to defiant hope, can enable us to recognize the force of Kevin Ellis's description of God in this book as disabled, a God not of power but of love. And the verses in which the psalmist speaks of God as a midwife: 'It is you that took me out of the womb: and laid me safe upon my mother's breast' (Psalm 22.9–10 CW) may well, as John Goldingay has pointed out, have evoked for Jesus his experience of being the child of Mary.[212]

Several other points are briefly worth noting. First, the Psalm moves from the individual to the corporate, from the present to the future, from despair to hope. But this is no easy transition: the articulation of despair and isolation, using imagery of the utmost directness and honesty, is alone what makes such a move possible. In some psalms, such a move can happen only fitfully; in others, such as Psalm 88, it does not happen at all.

---

210 Mark 15.34.

211 Psalm 22.8 and 22.18; cf. Matthew 27.43; John 19.24.

212 John Goldingay, *Psalms Volume 1: Psalms 1–41*, Baker Academic, 2006, p. 342.

Here, it is the result not only of feeling safe to lament and protest, but also of the psalmist's deliberate contrasting of his or her present predicament with the faith and experience of God's people: 'Our forebears trusted in you; they trusted, and you delivered them.' Part of the psalmist's response to terrible and inexplicable suffering is to dig deep into the faith tradition in which he or she stands in the urgent search for meaning and hope. That tradition is then set in direct collision with what is happening now: 'they' becomes 'I': 'as for me, I am a worm and no man: scorned by all and despised by the people', and the perfect tense (used in Hebrew to describe actions that have been completed) is replaced by the imperfect or present tense, with the language of faith and piety being subverted by vivid and violent animal imagery: 'The hounds are all about me, the pack of evildoers close in on me: they pierce my hands and my feet.' In other words: What is happening, Lord? Why has so promising a past, so strong a sense of corporate and personal vocation, led to such pointless suffering?

Second, Psalm 22 is not all prayer, in the sense of being addressed directly to God: after the long and desperate prayer for help to a God who has become both silent and distant: 'I cry in the daytime, but you do not answer . . . Be not far from me, O Lord' (Psalm 22.2,19 CW), the psalmist begins, with a new sense of hope, to speak *about* God to others, 'Praise the Lord, you that fear him . . . the poor shall eat and be satisfied'(Psalm 22.23–6 CW). This movement, from prayer to testimony and back again, happens constantly in the psalms and underlines the way that their spirituality can embrace much more of life than the more narrowly focused devotionalism of later generations. Some psalms are not strictly prayers at all: Psalm 82 visualizes God calling a tribunal to pronounce judgement on corrupt political leaders, only turning to urgent prayer in the final verse: the psalmist's dream or imaginative vision is finally addressed to God directly. In others, such as the famous Psalm 23, the movement is from personal reflection to prayer; the use of earthy rural imagery in the first part gives the psalmist permission, so to speak, to use similar imagery in the prayer that follows, imagining a God who lays a picnic table in immediate sight of the psalmist's enemies, thereby defying and deriding them. Psalm 73 begins with theology – talking about God – which is immediately subverted by the harsh reality of everyday life: only when the psalmist takes the sense of bafflement and outrage to which this gives rise *into the sanctuary* and prays with it does he or she discover, not so much an easy answer, as a profound and intimate sense of the divine presence.

The journey made by the person praying Psalm 22 is a long one. It begins, as we have seen, with agonized prayer that takes the form of questions addressed to God: 'why have you forsaken me, and are so far from my salvation, from the words of my distress?' Present suffering is at once compared with past blessings, after which lonely prayer ('Be not far from me, for trouble is near at hand: and there is none to help') leads to a vivid description of what is happening. Then, suddenly and unexpectedly, the psalmist moves to praise, anticipating and even celebrating now the new future he or she longs for God to bring to birth ('I will tell of your name to my people: in the midst of the congregation will I praise you'). Is this an easy piety, tacked on to an otherwise awkward prayer of protest? No: it is defiance of the status quo, a courageous envisioning of a radically different future even when – in fact precisely when – there is neither sign nor likelihood of that future ever coming to be. This is staring evil and adversity directly in the face and declaring, without any shred of evidence for doing so, that it will not, ever, have the last word. The psalm ends with a vision of a new future for the world: 'all the ends of the earth shall remember and turn to the Lord . . . declaring that he, the Lord, has done it.'

What has made the difference? Why this abrupt change in tone? The likeliest explanation is simply that the psalmist has felt heard, the Lord 'has not despised nor abhorred the suffering of the poor, neither has he hidden his face from them: but when they cried to him he heard them'. Prayers of lament such as this are not merely psychological wish-fulfilment, or a taking refuge in someone else's piety. They represent a paradox: on the one hand, a courageous willingness to stare suffering in the face, to describe it with unsparing honesty, and to let it collide head-on with previous experiences of faith – and, on the other hand, a refusal simply to submit to what is happening, a decision to *adapt* to but not to *conform* to the reality of suffering. This decision is made by someone no longer in control of what is happening to them. It is not a sudden access of energy and hope from within, or a brief but fruitless optimism. It is an act of faith, but perhaps even more of childlike trust, as though to say 'this is not how things should be' – and to discover, in the very act of saying it, that someone is listening.

It is not always that easy. Some lament psalms struggle to hold on to any sense of future hope; some (supremely Psalm 88) find no hope for the future at all. But even then, in the very act of giving expression to what is happening *now*, and comparing it with how things once were *then*, the possibility, however remote, of a different *tomorrow* may begin to emerge. And if it doesn't, or if we simply cannot conceive how it might, it remains important to *bear witness* to what has happened or is happening now. These great prayers exist because someone, somewhere, refused to collude with apathy and despair in the face of the gross and random reality of suffering. In her powerful study of the book of Lamentations, Maureen O'Connor writes:

> [The Book of] Lamentations urges us to do the difficult work of reclaiming our passion for life, for justice and empathy. Without such work we will never be able to hear the cries of the poor in our neighbourhood or around the globe.[213]

In short, lament can lift me out of me, out of an understandable but ultimately stifling self-preoccupation, to glimpse a wider view. This is how God answers the anguished prayers of Job, improbably inviting that agonized victim of unjust suffering

213 Maureen O'Connor, *Lamentations and the Tears of the World*, Orbis, 2002, p. xiv.

to consider the ostrich (Job 39.13–8), or the hippopotamus (Job 40.15–24), not from some ill-conceived sentimentality, but precisely in order to say to Job: I hear you; I made you; I care about you; but I need you to hear that there is more to life than what you can see of it. In short, it is only when, as Christopher Collingwood puts it in this book, we manage to let go of our separable external ego and embrace the reality of our true selves and of the world, as it truly is, that we begin to find a way forward.

Underlying the biblical prayer of lament is a memory of more than simply blessings in the past, or even of a sense of vocation which appears to have been cruelly subverted. Israel believed that God had initiated a covenant with her, that God and Israel together had entered into a lifelong nuptial relationship – and it is precisely this belief that allows the psalmist to bring all of his or her experience of life, including the hard questions, into that relationship: just as the child who believes itself to be unconditionally loved by its parents will similarly feel free to be transparently honest with them, rather than simply have to tell them what they want to hear. It is because of the covenant, because at some deep and corporate level Israel felt it was, or had been, loved and called, that its prayers give expression to almost every conceivable aspect of human experience, from passionate longing and wild celebration to furious anger and envy. Contributors to this book reiterate the critical importance, in times of terrible suffering, of knowing or believing yourself to be unconditionally loved; and the surest manifestation of that love is a sense that you are free to fail, or doubt, or challenge, and still be loved. It is just that deep corporate sense of *being loved* that freed Israel to bring all of life into its relationship with God. And a pattern of prayer or worship that does not give expression to that fundamental freedom fails to do justice to the God both of Israel and of Jesus Christ. Even more: like parents whose love for their children is unconditional, not dependent on the child's performance or behaviour, God comes closer when Israel screams or cries out or asks hard questions; it is no coincidence that one of the greatest prayers of lament, Psalm 73, ends with one of the most moving expressions of childlike trust and intimacy to be found in the Hebrew scriptures:

> Yet I am always with you:
> you hold me by my right hand.
> You will guide me with your counsel:
> and afterwards receive me with glory.
> Whom have I in heaven but you?
> And there is nothing upon earth that I desire in comparison with you. (Psalm 73.23–5 CW)

'. . . And afterwards receive me with glory.' With these words Psalm 73 trembles on the verge of a theology of resurrection. It is no more than the verge; but it reminds us of another reason why the great prayers of lament matter, a reason which brings us back to David Ford's words with which we began. They stretch and transform our theology. They can even take us to the brink of atheism: Samuel Balentine has written that

> perhaps the greatest irony of the biblical witness, and perhaps also its most impenetrable legacy of prayer, is that when one loses faith in God, it is precisely to God that one turns.[214]

We can see this in the way Psalm 73 begins: not with prayer, but with a piece of conventional theology which is instantly subverted by the harsh reality of the psalmist's own experience of life:

> Truly, God is loving to Israel:
> to those who are pure in heart.
> Nevertheless, my feet were almost gone:
> my steps had well-nigh slipped.
> For I was envious of the proud;
> I saw the wicked in such prosperity . . .

214 Samuel Balentine, *Prayer in the Hebrew Bible*, Fortress, 1993, p. 294.

Not only do the wicked do well for themselves ('they come to no misfortune like other folk') – they receive political honours and colossal salaries – but they tempt others to join them, and thereby challenge any belief in God:

> And so the people turn to them:
> and find in them no fault.
> They say, 'How should God know?
> Is there knowledge in the Most High?'
> (Psalm 73.10–11 CW)

It is only after the psalmist has explored the full implications of this gross injustice, only after he or she has begun to wonder whether there is a God there at all, that he or she turns to prayer. Other psalms scream at God to wake up: 'Rise up! Why sleep, O Lord?' (Psalm 44.24 CW); one describes God as a soldier with a bad hangover, 'Then the Lord awoke as out of sleep: like a warrior who has been overcome with wine' (Psalm 78.65 CW). This is not the language of polite Anglican collects, which evoke the beauty of holiness but run the risk of sending God back to sleep. The experience of suffering or injustice demands a more robust spirituality than that, and in turn can help us nurture a more robust theology. The German Catholic theologian Johann Baptist Metz called for a revitalization of the biblical language we have lost:

> Speaking about God always stems from speaking to God; theology comes from the language of prayer. That sounds pious and subjects me . . . to the suspicion that I, the political theologian, have made another turnabout, this time to piety and pious submission. But let us make no mistake: the language of prayer is not only more universal, but also more exciting and dramatic, much more rebellious and radical, than the language of current theology. It is much more disturbing, much more unconsoled, much less harmonious than that.[215]

215 From Johann Baptist Metz, 'Gotteskrise', in Eric Zenger, *A God of Vengeance: Understanding the Psalms of Divine Wrath*, trans. Linda M. Maloney, Westminster John Knox, 1996, p. 95.

The prayer of lament, then, is much more than a cosy escape into fantasy for the pious, or even for the desperate. It allows us (to use Rachel Lewis' image in this book) to begin the process of gathering up the scattered pieces of our souls; it enables us to look directly into the reality of suffering with the unconditioned directness of Peter Kerr's ten-year-old daughter. Furthermore, it equips us to challenge the injustices and question the evils of our world in a way that many cannot risk doing, and thereby to hasten the day when they can. One final theologian, Walter Brueggemann, deserves quotation:

> A community of faith which negates laments soon concludes that the hard issues of justice are improper questions to pose at the throne [of God], because the throne seems to be only a place of praise. I believe it thus follows that if justice questions are improper questions at the throne (which is a conclusion drawn through liturgic use), they soon appear to be improper questions in public places, in schools, in hospitals, with the government, and eventually even in the courts. Justice questions disappear into civility and docility. The order of the day comes to seem absolute, beyond question, and we are left with only grim obedience and eventually despair. The point of access for serious change has been forfeited when the propriety of this speech form is denied.[216]

How to use laments? We can pray them for ourselves. We can use them to enter imaginatively, and sensitively, into the experience of others, thereby enabling our prayers of intercession to go deeper than the effortless canter through the world's current trouble spots which can all too easily characterize them. In Jewish tradition, Psalm 22 is the prayer of Esther, the queen who suddenly finds her world turned upside down and her life endangered. But it could make just as much sense as the prayer of many of the contributors to this book. Psalm 55 can be read

216 Walter Brueggemann, 'The Costly Loss of Lament', in *Journal for the Study of the Old Testament* 36, 1986, p. 64.

as the prayer of a victim of rape, Psalm 58 as the prayer of those who have been brutalized by unspeakable evil, Psalm 3 as the prayer of an aid worker seized and held hostage by pitiless fundamentalists – and so on. And we can create our own laments, drawing on the rich interplay of experience, emotion, imagery, theology and prayer that characterize those in scripture. We can act, or sing, or paint them – or use them to enter, with Kevin Ellis in this book, into the mysterious dance of life. Above all, we can worship with them, thereby ensuring that all of our lives are given truthful and, finally, hopeful expression before the throne of God.

Index

Acceptance 21
Advent 99
Alcuin of York 49
Anderson, Bernard 16
Angel 154
Anger 28, 81
Anoint 121
Apocalypse 102
Aquinas, Thomas 184
Atkinson, David 8

Balaam's Ass 30
Bailey, Simon 13
Baisley, Barbara 10, 11, 21, 22
Barren 134
Bell, Rob 58
Biopsy 63
Bishop 52, 165, 172
Blind 5
Blood transfusion 149
Body 88, 118, 151, 152, 154
Bosworth, F. F. 7
Brain 25, 48
Bronze Serpent 92, 101, 110, 111, 112
Bruggemann, Walter 198

Cancer 2, 8, 9, 23, 28, 41, 53, 61, 64, 65, 73, 94, 114, 115, 116, 117, 119, 121, 123, 125, 126, 127, 128, 148, 151, 157, 158, 164, 166, 170, 171, 174, 175, 176, 179, 180, 181, 182
Casson, James 7
Cerebral haemorrhage 28
Chaos 77
Chicken, Peter 9
Childlessness 129, 131, 133, 136, 137, 138, 139, 143, 145
Chemotherapy 148, 157, 172, 175, 176
Clendinnen, Inga 19, 20, 21, 22
CLL 148, 157
Cloud of forgetting 20
Cobb, Mark 22
Coma 176
Comfort 69
Communion 154
Compassion 90, 182
Conflict 80
Consolation 115
Contemplative Prayer 102
Counsellor 83
Cross 1
Crucified 105, 178
Cry 84, 119, 127
Cure 3, 160

Dance 129, 134, 139, 145, 199
Dark Night of the Soul 72, 94, 149
Death 3, 37, 39, 49, 54, 61, 95, 99, 107, 120, 144, 149, 150, 166, 177
De Mello, Anthony 7, 8
Dependence 71

Depression 13, 45, 51, 75, 79, 155
Despair 67, 182, 185
Diagnosis 115
Disabled 141, 191
Disease 146
Distress 109
Doubt 7

Ego 105, 106, 107, 108, 110, 195
Eiesland, N. L. 140, 141
Emotion 46, 47, 48, 107, 109
Eucharist 83, 112, 113, 124, 182

Failure 94
Faith 25, 71, 91, 125
Fall 104
Fear 19, 119, 184
Ford, David 184
Forgiveness 62
Freedom 71

Gethsemane 10, 14
Grieving 2, 15
Griffiths, Bede 104
Good Friday 14
Grace 75, 81
Guilt 45, 46, 151, 167

Haemorrhage 131
Hallucination 20
Hardy, Daniel 3
Healing 1, 3, 4, 8, 9, 43, 45, 117, 150, 160, 174
Heart 37, 46, 47, 48, 77, 81, 83, 88
Heart attack 25, 28
Herbert, George 25, 30, 35, 36
Hillesum, Etty 82
Hinduism 102
HIV 13, 179
Hope 54, 144, 192, 194
Hopewell, James F. 23
Hospice 23, 54, 60
Hughes, Trystan O. 20
Hull, John 1, 18
Huntington's Disease 95, 96, 97, 100, 110
Hydronatremia 176
Hymns 77, 119, 124

ICD 40, 41
Impotent 134, 145
Ignatius 54
Infertility 129, 131, 132, 133, 135, 137

Jairus 185
Jesus prayer 39, 64
Jewish 90
Job 15, 55, 60, 65, 71, 178, 190, 194
John of the Cross 72
Judgement 71
Julian of Norwich 12, 30, 119
Jung 88

Kroll, Una 58
Kubler-Ross, Elizabeth 15, 16
Kushner, Harold 12

Lament 188, 190, 194, 195, 198
Lazarus 22
Leukaemia 146, 148, 150, 154, 157
Love 177, 191
Luther, Martin 184

Mammogram 169
Mansfield Katherine 16
Mastectomy 171, 179

Matthews, Caitlin 133
Mayne, Michael 11, 14, 18, 19, 20, 23, 58, 124, 126, 128
McCloughry, Roy 133
McCrum, Robert 2
ME 20
Merton, Thomas 155
Mercy 90
Metaphor 6, 18, 19, 36, 47
Metz, Johann Baptist 197
Midwife/midwifery 61, 62
Mind 118
Miracle 8, 43, 67, 74, 160, 183
Miscarriage 39, 50, 51, 52, 55, 56, 59, 60
Mortality 73
Mouth 70
MRI 65, 66
Music 19, 23, 27, 45, 91, 179, 187, 188

Narrative 23
Newman, John Henry 160
Nouwen, Henri 164

O'Connor, Flannery 159
O'Siadhail, Michael 162
Offices (Daily), 20, 115, 120, 123, 139
Orthodox 50, 90
Oxymoron 19

Pacemaker 40
Pain 44, 56, 68, 89, 93, 182
Palliative care 22
Panic 77
Parable 18
Patchwork 182
Peace 37
Physical 109
Piper Alpha 187
Powerless 94
Prayer 25, 27, 34, 35, 42, 43, 51, 65, 68, 73, 91, 117, 122, 125, 173, 174, 190, 195
Pregnancy 53
Priest 9, 98, 111, 112, 115, 127, 132, 139, 145, 146, 169, 170, 171, 172, 183
Projection 167
Psalm 17, 18, 39, 47, 52, 69, 120, 124, 148, 151, 154, 155, 156, 181, 185, 190, 191, 192, 194, 196
Psyche 98
Psychosomatic 100
Psychotherapy 88
Public representative 159, 163, 185

Radiotherapy 65, 66, 123, 126
Rape 97
Reason 47
Reconciliation 182
Redemption 150
Reflection 68
Relational/relationship 30, 63, 71, 91, 150
Remission 148, 159, 160, 181
Respite 75
Resurrection 5, 30, 112, 142
Retreat 89
Revelation 102
Ritual 16, 17
Rose, Gillian 19, 21, 22

Sacraments 23
Sacred 146
Salvation 145
Sanctus 39

Saunders, Cicely 23
Scapegoat 189
Self 72, 90, 102, 103, 104, 105, 106, 107, 118, 195
Shadow 113
Shock 170
Silence 157
Sleep 82
Soelle, Dorothee 16
Sontag, Susan 6
Soul 81,90
Spirit 6, 30, 35, 88, 101, 118, 151
Spiritual 46, 88, 94, 109
Spiritual care 83
Spleen 153
Spufford, Margaret 11, 14, 19
Stages of grieving/fear 19, 21, 125
Stancliffe, David 2, 4
Sterile 134
Stillbirth 52
Storytelling 23
Stories 89
Stress 81
Stroke 2, 25, 27, 28, 30, 35
Suffering 56, 58, 60, 70, 71, 73, 100, 126, 141, 184

Tapestry 61, 165
Terminal 21, 146
Tertullian 186
Thanksgiving 69
Theresa of Avila 34
Thinking 30
Thomas, R. S. 178
Thought 47
Time 1, 85, 91, 156
Tiredness 28
Toothache 63
Transformation 21, 99, 127
Truth 110
Tumour 74

Unconscious 99, 100, 101, 106
Understanding 69

Vulnerable 50
Vocation 146, 159, 160

Walter, Tony 16
Warnock, Mary 135
Watson, David 8, 10, 147
Wholeness 22, 24
Wilderness 108
Williams, Rowan 134, 144
Withdrawal/absence of God 27

Young, Frances 12

Zen 102, 103, 104